SAXOPHONE UNIVERSITY

A Comprehensive Resource for the
Developing Saxophone Musician

BY **UELI DÖRIG**

Illustrations by Alice Zhang

ISBN 978-1-4950-9148-3

HAL•LEONARD®
7777 W. BLUEMOUND RD. P.O. BOX 13819 MILWAUKEE, WI 53213

In Australia Contact:
Hal Leonard Australia Pty. Ltd.
4 Lentara Court
Cheltenham, Victoria, 3192 Australia
Email: ausadmin@halleonard.com.au

Visit Hal Leonard Online at
www.halleonard.com

For Margot & Loup

ACKNOWLEDGMENTS

I'd like to thank my parents Irene & Hansi who deeply understand the benefits of a great education and always supported me in my journeys and endeavors.

A great thank you goes to Alice Zhang who did the wonderful drawings that you will find throughout the book.

It was a great pleasure to work with Matt Wolf and the Hal Leonard staff. Thanks guys for all your hard work and invaluable guidance!

Last but not least, I'd like to thank my beautiful wife Claudia. Je t'aime mon amour!

TABLE OF CONTENTS

PART 3: PRACTICE TOOLBOX

PAGE FINDERS

Cut the page finders out, fold them in the middle and tape them on the beginning of each matching chapter, so the space with the text is visible when the book is closed.

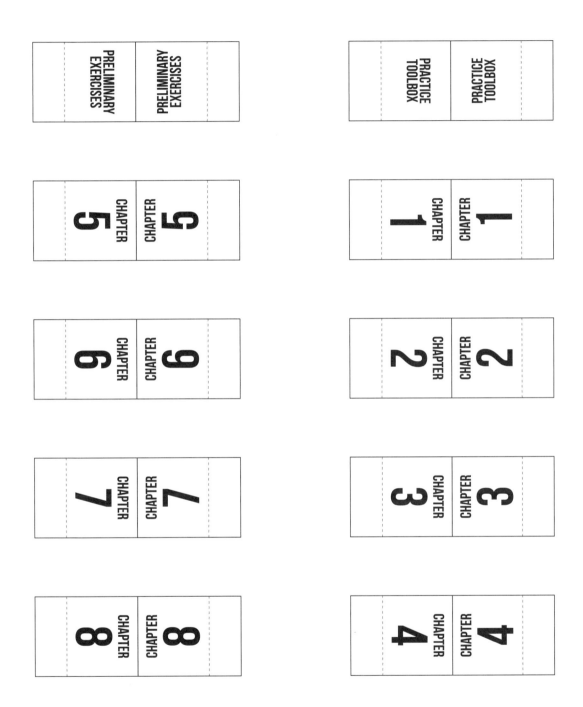

INTRODUCTION

HOW TO USE THIS BOOK

Take your time. Try to play everything with the best sound possible. Play everything slowly at first. If something is too difficult, slow it down. To learn new information, great players slow everything down to a point where they can control every musical element (i.e. fingerings, rhythm, articulation, dynamics, style, etc.). Once that is taken care of, then gradually speed it up to the desired tempo.

Internalize all exercises in all twelve keys.

Memorization is part of internalization, but "internalize" really means to know and to understand the information. Therefore, internalization goes beyond memorization.

People who tend to practice technique over musicianship end up sounding like a robot, so please do not use this book exclusively. It is very important to include something that is fun to play in every practice session.

The natural minor scale is being treated in this book as the Aeolian mode of a major scale (a major scale started on its sixth scale degree). However, the natural minor scale however doesn't come up anywhere in this book. Harmonic and melodic minor, on the other hand, have been included in the scale exercises as they add a completely different flavor or taste. Note that melodic minor is sometimes also referred to as "jazz minor" or "real minor."

There are practice logs provided to keep track of your progress. Make your check marks with pencil, so you can use this book more than once.

To get most out of this book I recommend having someone involved who regularly checks your progress. Ideally, this would be a qualified music teacher.

WHY GOOD TECHNIQUE IS IMPORTANT

Good technique doesn't necessarily make you a good player, but every good player has good technique. Good technique is like having a solid foundation. If you want to grow tall, it is essential to have a solid foundation.

ATTITUDE

The following is a list of thoughts that helped me develop a good work discipline. They also offered me some guidance in times when I questioned myself.

· Music is extremely honest and fair. You cannot buy technique, creativity, or artistry. These aspects are only available through hard work.

· If someone is a better player than you, he or she has probably worked harder and/or longer.

· There will always be someone who plays better than you do. Don't worry about it. Accept it and focus on being the best player you can be.

· Meeting a better player is a good thing! Don't look down on yourself. Figure out "what does he or she do better than I do?" You also want to ask yourself "how can I get there?"

· You cannot be over-prepared.

10 DO'S AND DON'TS OF PRACTICING THE SAXOPHONE

1. Stand or sit straight, but stay relaxed.

2. To learn something efficiently, learn it in this order:
   a. Concentrate on the fingerings
   b. Deal with the rhythm
   c. Add the correct articulation and dynamics
   d. Adjust tempo/speed. This always comes last.

3. Have the patience to slow things down. You achieve accuracy and precision with a slow tempo.

4. Don't always play the whole tune or exercise from beginning to end. It is much more time-efficient to deal with problems directly. First isolate and correct a problem, then put it back into its context.

5. Use your ears: listen to what you are playing. Record yourself from time to time and analyze your sound, rhythm/time, phrasing, accuracy, etc.

6. Learn scales using the entire range of your instrument. This way, the very high and low notes of your saxophone will become much less intimidating.

7. Keep your fingers close to the keys. This will make playing fast much easier and smoother. It also eliminates the chances of your fingers going to the wrong place.

8. Breath support comes from your diaphragm (use your belly and not your mouth to build up air pressure).

9. Be prepared and be confident. Then you will sound confident!

10. For every hour you practice, listen to great saxophone players for two hours. Section 9.5 of this book will help you find players to check out.

HOW TO PRACTICE SCALES

You can't play something too slowly. If you play something fast but wrong ten times in a row, you are just reinforcing bad habits. Listen carefully to what you are doing. Be sure you understand the information you want to learn. Know the scale in your mind and focus on each note as you play it. Practice slowly at first and only bring the tempo up when you are comfortable. Remember, the quality of your practice session will be very low if you increase the tempo before you know the material 100%. You want to aim for accuracy – don't settle for anything but perfection. Learn to listen to yourself and always check if the quality of what you are doing meets the highest standards.

USING THE PIANO AS A PRACTICE TOOL

The piano is helpful for learning music theory, and especially for learning modes, arpeggios, and chords. For example, we cannot play the different notes of a chord at the same time with a saxophone, but with a piano this is rather easy. Another advantage of using the piano as a practice tool is that you can see the notes on the keyboard. If you are a visual person, playing the piano will help you even more. Every musician, regardless of his principal instrument, should have at least some basic piano skills.

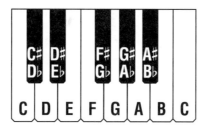

Ex. 1 Piano keyboard (one octave)

We don't have to focus on breathing and sound production while playing the piano, which leaves us more brainpower to focus on internalizing the scales, modes, arpeggios, and chords. Therefore, using a piano as a practice tool is a great shortcut that comes with many other benefits.

The design of a piano keyboard is helpful to demonstrate the whole and half steps between the notes of a scale. As it turns out, we are always dealing with the same twelve notes. It is the way we arrange these notes (using different whole step and half step combinations) that distinguishes the different scales.

USING A METRONOME AS A PRACTICE TOOL

Using a metronome can be a great deal of help. However, if the metronome has been set to too fast a tempo, it will create an atmosphere of stress. You want to set the tempo to a challenging, yet manageable tempo. Only increase speed when you can play it 100% correctly.

Try to use the metronome on different beats (on x):

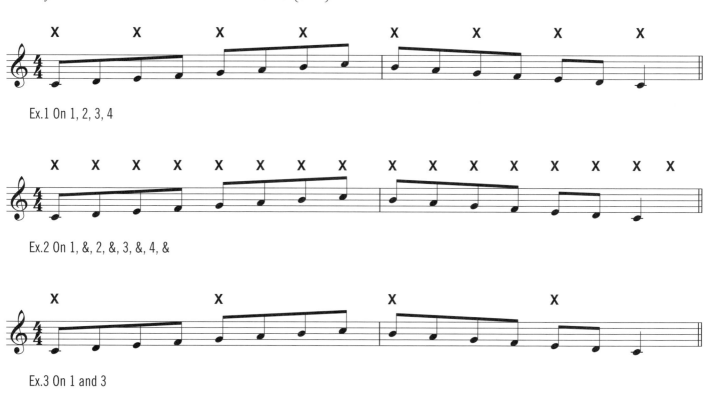

Ex.1 On 1, 2, 3, 4

Ex.2 On 1, &, 2, &, 3, &, 4, &

Ex.3 On 1 and 3

Ex.4 On 2 and 4

PART 1:
PRELIMINARY EXERCISES

SOUND QUALITY EXERCISE

A good sound is of primary importance. It won't matter how complicated a line you play, if you have a bad sound, no one will enjoy listening to your playing. On the other hand, you can capture an audience with just one long note if it is played correctly.

To do so, it is helpful to have a visual idea of how a perfect note (short or long) looks like. Every note has three parts:

1. beginning

2. duration

3. end

A well-controlled note has a clear beginning, duration, and end.

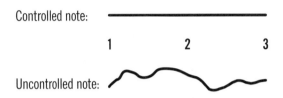

A poor note lacks a clear and strong beginning. It does whatever it wants during the long or short time it is held. Finally, there is no clear end to the note – it simply fades out.

Control the beginning

Use your tongue to control the beginning of a note. Tongue "TA" to get a sharp beginning, or tongue "DA" to start the note softly. In both ways, it is you who decides when the note starts, not your saxophone.

Control the duration

To make the duration of a note look like a straight line you need to control the air stream. The air pressure needs to be constant as long as the note sounds. To do this, you need to control the air stream with your diaphragm.

Control the end

The end of a note is the easiest part to control. Nevertheless, it is often the most neglected part of the three and you can hear it immediately if a player is aware of it or not. Knowing how to control the end of a note makes the difference between an okay player and a great player. If you want to control the end of a note, put your tongue back on the reed to stop the vibration.

Once you can play a nice, strong, and controlled sounding note with ease, you're ready to take on all the notes of your saxophone. Start in the middle range of the saxophone and gradually expand your comfort zone towards the very high and low notes.

The next step is to vary the dynamics. Play all the notes quietly at first, then later at a louder volume (don't change the volume while playing). High notes sound louder on the saxophone. Therefore, to make a scale sound even, you need to slightly cut back the volume on the very high notes, without losing the sound quality. Take your time!

TUNING EXERCISE

Intonation (the ability to play in tune) is an important element of playing the saxophone.

There are two ways to address intonation. You can either tune with your ear or with an electronic tuner. I prefer tuning my saxophone with my ear. Although it takes more training, you really don't want to depend on a tuner all the time. You never know when a tuner will stop working (probably when you need it most). Another reason I prefer to tune by ear is because of the nature of the saxophone. It is quite difficult (if not impossible) for the saxophone to be perfectly in tune from top to bottom. Once you tune a certain range of the saxophone, you might find another range is now out of tune. There are certain additional factors (i.e. temperature) that make the saxophone difficult to tune. As a saxophone warms up, it will tend to play sharper. As a saxophonist, you must learn to listen to this and make the necessary adjustments. Also, if you play in a situation where the rest of the band plays either sharp or flat, your tuner will not help you at all. For all these reasons, I recommend you approach tuning and intonation with your ears and not with a machine.

Having said that, it helps to know the intonation tendencies of your saxophone. After you have established a nice sound on your horn, you want to get together with a friend and a good tuner that reads sound on a Hertz (Hz) number scale. Don't use a tuner that only uses red and green lights, as they are not accurate enough. If you don't have a tuner yet, you can easily find a tuner application for your smartphone, tablet, or computer. Your friend will call out all the notes on your saxophone, but out of order. As you play each note as a well-controlled long note, he or she will log the results on a piece of paper. If you do this several times and analyze the results, you will discover which notes tend to be sharp or flat and by how much. If you are an experienced saxophone player with good ears, your notes shouldn't be more than three or four Hz off.

LONG TONE CHAMPIONSHIP

All you need do for this exercise is to take a deep breath and to play a note as long as humanly possible. STOP DOING THIS IF YOU START FEELING DIZZY!

The long tone championship exercise will help you have a better understanding of the relationship between your body and your instrument. A saxophone player needs to understand and control his/her body as much as his/her horn.

This brings us to three interesting questions:

1. What note should we play?

2. How do we play that note?

3. What is the best way to inhale the most air?

1. What note should we play?
As a rule, the more fingers that are pressing down keys, the further the air stream has to be pushed. Therefore, the more fingers you press, the bigger the effort is to play that note. For this exercise, we like easy. So play a note that involves no or few fingers.

Comfort is important for this. Many saxophone players like G and have the best results using it. They should do better with C#, but comfort outweighs logic.

2. How do we play?
Can you play longer with a screaming loud sound or just a whistle? This is not a beauty contest; play as quietly as you can. However, the danger with soft notes is that you will cut the air stream and lose the sound of your note. The long tone championship is a great exercise for airstream control.

3. What is the best way to inhale the most air?
Picture two chambers in your body where you can put air: your belly and your chest. If you fill up your belly first and then continue with your chest, you get the maximum capacity. If you start with your chest first, then you block the belly chamber. Try to relax as much as possible.

Time yourself and try to gradually increase the duration of your notes. Good luck!

DONKEY EXERCISE

There is a problem that occurs when saxophone players leap from a high note to a low note. If both notes lack control, we get a sound like a donkey shouting ("hee-haw"). This loss in sound quality will become apparent once you start working on the scale exercises with diatonic intervals in chapters 3 through 7. As a preparation exercise, play notes in the high register and then quickly play the same note again an octave below. Try to sound like a donkey first and then do it again without sounding like a donkey.

OVERCOMING THE OCTAVE BREAK

A special situation occurs when we slur from a note with few fingers involved like C, to a note with many fingers involved like D.

There is a lot of finger action happening when we go from a fingering like C, B, or C♯ to a fingering like D, D♯, or E. This action often interrupts the air stream while playing with soft dynamics, meaning you lose your sound if you don't support your air stream enough when going from C to D. To overcome this, push the airstream a bit with your diaphragm at the precise moment when you go from a note with few fingers to a note with many fingers. This will fix the problem.

TONGUING EXERCISE

This exercise helps you to get:

1. Better control of the release of notes.

2. Better and bigger sound.

3. The capability to play effortlessly for a long time.

Exercise

Procedure

1. Play the above two measures in an endless loop.

2. Use a metronome and start at a slow tempo (around 60 bpm, or beats per minute).

3. Play loudly and staccato, but stay relaxed.

4. Focus on producing the necessary air support with your diaphragm. Push a little with your diaphragm for each note.

5. After each repetition move by a half step. Go up and down using the whole range of your instrument.

6. Remember to relax your body as much as possible. Focus on lightening the tongue action.

7. Once you have practiced the exercise on the entire range of the saxophone, speed the metronome up by 20 bpm. Only increase the tempo if the quality of what you are hearing is more than acceptable.

8. Go faster and faster.

VIBRATO EXERCISE

1. Use a metronome at a very slow tempo (40 bpm) and play any note you want as a long note.

2. Push the airstream with your diaphragm at each click (be as accurate as possible). You are doing it correctly when your note gets a little louder at each click.

3. Do two pushes per beat, like playing eighth notes.

4. Do three pushes per beat, like playing eighth note triplets.

5. Do four pushes per beat, like playing sixteenth notes.

6. Set the metronome at a faster tempo and repeat steps 2 through 5.

7. Speed up again and again but never neglect accuracy to achieve speed.

8. Do the vibrato exercise using all notes of your saxophone.

Any note being played with vibrato should start with the most air support and then diminish a bit. Never start a vibrato quietly and get louder.

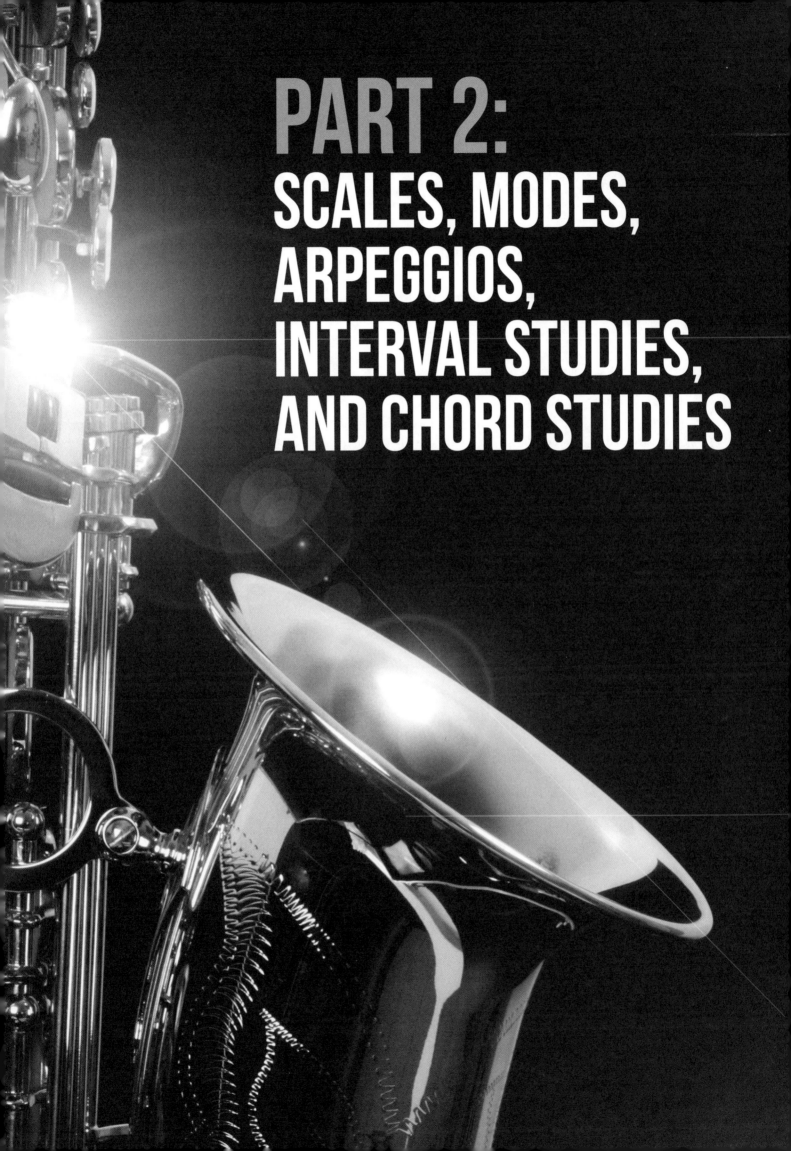

PART 2:
SCALES, MODES, ARPEGGIOS, INTERVAL STUDIES, AND CHORD STUDIES

CHAPTER 1

1.1. THEORY: MAJOR SCALES

A major scale is made up of eight notes. The last note is the first note again but an octave higher, so there are seven different notes in a major scale. The first note gives the scale its name. Therefore, Ex. 1 is called a "C major scale."

Ex.1 Eight notes of the C major scale

All scales get their characteristic sound from the notes they are made of and the intervals (vertical space) between them. Ex. 2 shows the structure of all major scales. Whole or Half represents the whole or half step interval between the notes.

Ex.2 Whole/half step structure of a major scale

We can take this structure and use it as our recipe to create other major scales. Let's create the G major scale as an example:

Recipe:	W	W	H	W	W	W	H	
G Major Scale:	G	A	B	C	D	E	F♯	G

Observation: To follow the structure of the major scales we had to raise the seventh note by a half step (F becomes F♯).

Remember, you need to know all 12 major scales.

Tip: As mentioned in the introduction, a piano keyboard is a great tool to visualize the whole/half step structures of scales.

1.2. PLAY ALL 12 MAJOR SCALES WITH MIXED ARTICULATION

Articulation patterns

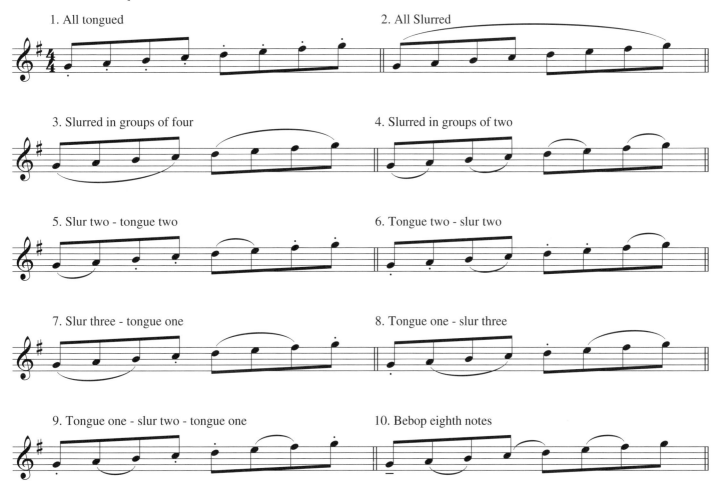

1. All tongued
2. All Slurred
3. Slurred in groups of four
4. Slurred in groups of two
5. Slur two - tongue two
6. Tongue two - slur two
7. Slur three - tongue one
8. Tongue one - slur three
9. Tongue one - slur two - tongue one
10. Bebop eighth notes

Tip: Always deal with one aspect at a time (i.e. fingerings, rhythm, articulation, or tempo). This enhances your chances to overcome an obstacle, and speeds up the learning process. Sing the articulation in your head before you start to play. Once you have memorized the feeling of a specific articulation, you are ready to play the scale. Focus on light use of the tongue and try to achieve the desired articulation with the smallest amount of tongue movement.

Scales should always be played on the entire range of your instrument. Play scales with an F♯/G♭ in them all the way up to high F♯/G♭, only if your saxophone has a high F♯ key. Playing scales on the entire range of the saxophone is a great way to expose you to the very high notes and the very low notes.

C Major

Don't forget to play the scales using different articulation patterns.

Major Scales Practice Log

Play all 12 major scales from ♪ = 60 to ♪ = 220.

	60	80	100	120	140	160	180	200	220
C									
G									
D									
A									
E									
B									
F♯/G♭									
D♭									
A♭									
E♭									
B♭									
F									

1.3. THEORY: MODES

There are seven modes in a major scale:

MODE:	EXAMPLE:	FORMULA:
1. Ionian	C D E F G A B C	W W H W W W H
2. Dorian	D E F G A B C D	W H W W W H W
3. Phrygian	E F G A B C D E	H W W W H W W
4. Lydian	F G A B C D E F	W W W H W W H
5. Mixolydian	G A B C D E F G	W W H W W H W
6. Aeolian	A B C D E F G A	W H W W H W W
7. Locrian	B C D E F G A B	H W W H W W W

The first mode (Ionian) is the same as a major scale. The second mode (Dorian) is a major scale started on its second note and ended on that note an octave higher. The third mode (Phrygian) starts on the third note, etc.

Every mode has a different sound or flavor to it. This is because every mode has a different formula.

We can take the formula of a mode and use it as our recipe to create a mode starting on a different note than the ones above. Let's create D Aeolian as an example:

Recipe for Aeolian:		W		H		W		W		H		W		W	
D Aeolian	D		E		F		G		A		B♭		C		D

1.4. PLAY ALL MODES OF ALL 12 MAJOR SCALES (ONE OCTAVE ONLY)

C Major Modes

MODE NUMBER		MODE NAME	SCALE RECIPE
1st mode	=	Ionian (Major)	= 1 2 3 4 5 6 7 8
2nd mode	=	Dorian	= 1 2 ♭3 4 5 6 ♭7 8
3rd mode	=	Phrygian	= 1 ♭2 ♭3 4 5 ♭6 ♭7 8
4th mode	=	Lydian	= 1 2 3 ♯4 5 6 7 8
5th mode	=	Mixolydian	= 1 2 3 4 5 6 ♭7 8
6th mode	=	Aeolian (Natural Minor)	= 1 2 ♭3 4 5 ♭6 ♭7 8
7th mode	=	Locrian	= 1 ♭2 ♭3 4 ♭5 ♭6 ♭7 8

Modes of the Major Scales Practice Log

Play all modes of all 12 major scales from ♪ = 60 to ♪ = 220.

	60		80		100		120		140		160		180		200		220	
C	Ion	Mix	Ion	Mix	Ion	Mix	Ion	Mix	Ion	Mix	Ion	Mix	Ion	Mix	Ion	Mix	Ion	Mix
	Dor	Aeo	Dor	Aeo	Dor	Aeo	Dor	Aeo	Dor	Aeo	Dor	Aeo	Dor	Aeo	Dor	Aeo	Dor	Aeo
	Phr	Loc	Phr	Loc	Phr	Loc	Phr	Loc	Phr	Loc	Phr	Loc	Phr	Loc	Phr	Loc	Phr	Loc
	Lyd		Lyd		Lyd		Lyd		Lyd		Lyd		Lyd		Lyd		Lyd	
G	Ion	Mix	Ion	Mix	Ion	Mix	Ion	Mix	Ion	Mix	Ion	Mix	Ion	Mix	Ion	Mix	Ion	Mix
	Dor	Aeo	Dor	Aeo	Dor	Aeo	Dor	Aeo	Dor	Aeo	Dor	Aeo	Dor	Aeo	Dor	Aeo	Dor	Aeo
	Phr	Loc	Phr	Loc	Phr	Loc	Phr	Loc	Phr	Loc	Phr	Loc	Phr	Loc	Phr	Loc	Phr	Loc
	Lyd		Lyd		Lyd		Lyd		Lyd		Lyd		Lyd		Lyd		Lyd	
D	Ion	Mix	Ion	Mix	Ion	Mix	Ion	Mix	Ion	Mix	Ion	Mix	Ion	Mix	Ion	Mix	Ion	Mix
	Dor	Aeo	Dor	Aeo	Dor	Aeo	Dor	Aeo	Dor	Aeo	Dor	Aeo	Dor	Aeo	Dor	Aeo	Dor	Aeo
	Phr	Loc	Phr	Loc	Phr	Loc	Phr	Loc	Phr	Loc	Phr	Loc	Phr	Loc	Phr	Loc	Phr	Loc
	Lyd		Lyd		Lyd		Lyd		Lyd		Lyd		Lyd		Lyd		Lyd	
A	Ion	Mix	Ion	Mix	Ion	Mix	Ion	Mix	Ion	Mix	Ion	Mix	Ion	Mix	Ion	Mix	Ion	Mix
	Dor	Aeo	Dor	Aeo	Dor	Aeo	Dor	Aeo	Dor	Aeo	Dor	Aeo	Dor	Aeo	Dor	Aeo	Dor	Aeo
	Phr	Loc	Phr	Loc	Phr	Loc	Phr	Loc	Phr	Loc	Phr	Loc	Phr	Loc	Phr	Loc	Phr	Loc
	Lyd		Lyd		Lyd		Lyd		Lyd		Lyd		Lyd		Lyd		Lyd	
E	Ion	Mix	Ion	Mix	Ion	Mix	Ion	Mix	Ion	Mix	Ion	Mix	Ion	Mix	Ion	Mix	Ion	Mix
	Dor	Aeo	Dor	Aeo	Dor	Aeo	Dor	Aeo	Dor	Aeo	Dor	Aeo	Dor	Aeo	Dor	Aeo	Dor	Aeo
	Phr	Loc	Phr	Loc	Phr	Loc	Phr	Loc	Phr	Loc	Phr	Loc	Phr	Loc	Phr	Loc	Phr	Loc
	Lyd		Lyd		Lyd		Lyd		Lyd		Lyd		Lyd		Lyd		Lyd	
B	Ion	Mix	Ion	Mix	Ion	Mix	Ion	Mix	Ion	Mix	Ion	Mix	Ion	Mix	Ion	Mix	Ion	Mix
	Dor	Aeo	Dor	Aeo	Dor	Aeo	Dor	Aeo	Dor	Aeo	Dor	Aeo	Dor	Aeo	Dor	Aeo	Dor	Aeo
	Phr	Loc	Phr	Loc	Phr	Loc	Phr	Loc	Phr	Loc	Phr	Loc	Phr	Loc	Phr	Loc	Phr	Loc
	Lyd		Lyd		Lyd		Lyd		Lyd		Lyd		Lyd		Lyd		Lyd	
F#/G♭	Ion	Mix	Ion	Mix	Ion	Mix	Ion	Mix	Ion	Mix	Ion	Mix	Ion	Mix	Ion	Mix	Ion	Mix
	Dor	Aeo	Dor	Aeo	Dor	Aeo	Dor	Aeo	Dor	Aeo	Dor	Aeo	Dor	Aeo	Dor	Aeo	Dor	Aeo
	Phr	Loc	Phr	Loc	Phr	Loc	Phr	Loc	Phr	Loc	Phr	Loc	Phr	Loc	Phr	Loc	Phr	Loc
	Lyd		Lyd		Lyd		Lyd		Lyd		Lyd		Lyd		Lyd		Lyd	
D♭	Ion	Mix	Ion	Mix	Ion	Mix	Ion	Mix	Ion	Mix	Ion	Mix	Ion	Mix	Ion	Mix	Ion	Mix
	Dor	Aeo	Dor	Aeo	Dor	Aeo	Dor	Aeo	Dor	Aeo	Dor	Aeo	Dor	Aeo	Dor	Aeo	Dor	Aeo
	Phr	Loc	Phr	Loc	Phr	Loc	Phr	Loc	Phr	Loc	Phr	Loc	Phr	Loc	Phr	Loc	Phr	Loc
	Lyd		Lyd		Lyd		Lyd		Lyd		Lyd		Lyd		Lyd		Lyd	
A♭	Ion	Mix	Ion	Mix	Ion	Mix	Ion	Mix	Ion	Mix	Ion	Mix	Ion	Mix	Ion	Mix	Ion	Mix
	Dor	Aeo	Dor	Aeo	Dor	Aeo	Dor	Aeo	Dor	Aeo	Dor	Aeo	Dor	Aeo	Dor	Aeo	Dor	Aeo
	Phr	Loc	Phr	Loc	Phr	Loc	Phr	Loc	Phr	Loc	Phr	Loc	Phr	Loc	Phr	Loc	Phr	Loc
	Lyd		Lyd		Lyd		Lyd		Lyd		Lyd		Lyd		Lyd		Lyd	
E♭	Ion	Mix	Ion	Mix	Ion	Mix	Ion	Mix	Ion	Mix	Ion	Mix	Ion	Mix	Ion	Mix	Ion	Mix
	Dor	Aeo	Dor	Aeo	Dor	Aeo	Dor	Aeo	Dor	Aeo	Dor	Aeo	Dor	Aeo	Dor	Aeo	Dor	Aeo
	Phr	Loc	Phr	Loc	Phr	Loc	Phr	Loc	Phr	Loc	Phr	Loc	Phr	Loc	Phr	Loc	Phr	Loc
	Lyd		Lyd		Lyd		Lyd		Lyd		Lyd		Lyd		Lyd		Lyd	
B♭	Ion	Mix	Ion	Mix	Ion	Mix	Ion	Mix	Ion	Mix	Ion	Mix	Ion	Mix	Ion	Mix	Ion	Mix
	Dor	Aeo	Dor	Aeo	Dor	Aeo	Dor	Aeo	Dor	Aeo	Dor	Aeo	Dor	Aeo	Dor	Aeo	Dor	Aeo
	Phr	Loc	Phr	Loc	Phr	Loc	Phr	Loc	Phr	Loc	Phr	Loc	Phr	Loc	Phr	Loc	Phr	Loc
	Lyd		Lyd		Lyd		Lyd		Lyd		Lyd		Lyd		Lyd		Lyd	
F	Ion	Mix	Ion	Mix	Ion	Mix	Ion	Mix	Ion	Mix	Ion	Mix	Ion	Mix	Ion	Mix	Ion	Mix
	Dor	Aeo	Dor	Aeo	Dor	Aeo	Dor	Aeo	Dor	Aeo	Dor	Aeo	Dor	Aeo	Dor	Aeo	Dor	Aeo
	Phr	Loc	Phr	Loc	Phr	Loc	Phr	Loc	Phr	Loc	Phr	Loc	Phr	Loc	Phr	Loc	Phr	Loc
	Lyd		Lyd		Lyd		Lyd		Lyd		Lyd		Lyd		Lyd		Lyd	

1.5. THEORY: TRIADS

Notes can be played (A) horizontally as a melody or scale, but they can also be played (B) vertically and create harmony. If at least two notes sound consecutively, we speak of a melody (it can even be the same note twice). If at least two notes sound at the same moment, we speak of harmony.

Playing harmony with a saxophone can mean two things:

A group of saxophone players play different notes at the same time to create harmony.

A saxophone player outlines harmony by playing the notes of the harmonic structure (i.e. triad) in order. Another word for outlining harmony this way is called playing "arpeggios." Arpeggios can be played straight or broken, as you will see in section 1.6.

A triad is a chord (set) of three notes. The three notes of a triad are stacked on top of each other so they all fall either on lines or on spaces. There are four different kinds of triads. The example bellow shows a C major triad (C), a C minor triad (Cm), a C augmented triad (C+), and a C diminished triad (C°). Capital "M" indicates an interval of a major third between two notes whereas a lower case "m" indicates an interval of a minor third between two notes.

C, Cm, C+, and C° are called chord symbols. It is important to understand chord symbols and what they represent.

The numbers in the above example represent the intervals between the three chord tones and the bottom note (C).

Triad inversions

We can change the structure of a triad in two ways. We can either put the second note on the bottom, or we can put the third note on the bottom. In all three examples, a different chord tone gets a chance to be in the bass. C/E indicates a C major chord with an E as the lowest note.

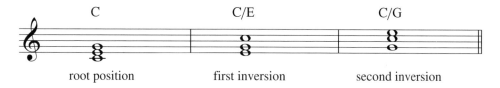

Tip: Use a piano to hear how triads sound and learn to recognize them with your ears.

Triad arpeggios

Because we can't play all three notes of a triad at the same time, we will play one note after the other. This is called playing an arpeggio.

1.6. PLAY ALL MAJOR TRIAD ARPEGGIOS (STRAIGHT AND BROKEN)

C Major Triad

Straight

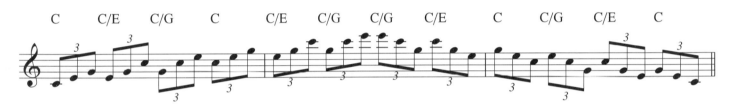

Broken in groups of three

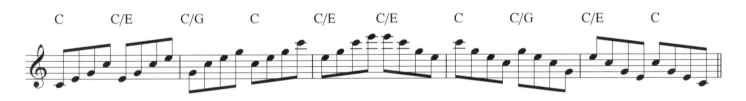

Broken in groups of four

Major Triad Arpeggios Practice Log

Play all major triad arpeggios from ♪ = 60 to ♪ = 220.

	60	80	100	120	140	160	180	200	220
C									
G									
D									
A									
E									
B									
F#/G♭									
D♭									
A♭									
E♭									
B♭									
F									

1.7. CHAPTER 1 RESEARCH ASSIGNMENTS

The chapter assignments should be a part of your weekly practice routine. Each square (below) equals one hour spent doing research. Copy the template "Analytical listening" in section 9.16. and use it for each player.

Watching (YouTube)

☐ ☐ ☐ ☐   Sidney Bechet

☐ ☐ ☐ ☐   Rahsaan Roland Kirk

☐ ☐ ☐ ☐   Grover Washington Jr.

☐ ☐ ☐ ☐   Bob Mintzer

☐ ☐ ☐ ☐   Kenny Garrett

Reading (Wikipedia, artist's website, saxophone websites, etc.)

☐ ☐   Sidney Bechet

☐ ☐   Rahsaan Roland Kirk

☐ ☐   Grover Washington Jr.

☐ ☐   Bob Mintzer

☐ ☐   Kenny Garrett

Listening (iTunes, public library, etc.)

☐ ☐ ☐   Sidney Bechet

☐ ☐ ☐   Rahsaan Roland Kirk

☐ ☐ ☐   Grover Washington Jr.

☐ ☐ ☐   Bob Mintzer

☐ ☐ ☐   Kenny Garrett

1.8. TEST: CHAPTER 1

Q1: What is the whole/half step structure of a major scale?

A1:

Q2: What is the second mode of a major scale called?

A2:

Q3: What is the sixth mode of a major scale called?

A3:

Q4: What are the notes of an E♭ major scale?

A4:

Q5: What are the notes of a B major scale?

A5:

Q6: What are the notes of a D Mixolydian scale?

A6:

Q7: What are the notes of an F Phrygian scale?

A7:

Q8: What are the notes in an F♯° triad?

A8:

Q9: What are the notes in a D♭+ triad?

A9:

Q10: What kind of an inversion is a G/D triad?

A10:

Do not continue with the next chapter before you have internalized everything from this chapter!

CHAPTER 2

2.1. THEORY: HARMONIC MINOR SCALES

Like the major scales, the harmonic minor scales are made up of eight notes. The difference is that in a harmonic minor scale, the third and sixth note get lowered by a half step.

Ex.1 Major scale

Ex. 2 Harmonic minor scale

Recipe to get a harmonic minor scale:
Take a major scale.
Lower the third and sixth notes by adding a flat or taking away a sharp.

Major:	D	E	F#	G	A	B	C#	D
Harmonic Minor:	D	E	F	G	A	B♭	C#	D

Ex. 3 D harmonic minor

It is important to understand that in this book, we will compare the structure (recipes) of all future scales to the structure of the major scale. You will need to know your major scales inside out to benefit the most from this book!

2.2. PLAY ALL 12 HARMONIC MINOR SCALES WITH MIXED ARTICULATION

Remember that scales should always be played on the entire range of your instrument.

The material in this book will contain double sharps and double flats from now on. A double sharp ("𝄪") brings a note a whole step up. A double flat ("♭♭") lowers a note a whole step.

C Harmonic Minor

Tip: You can review the instructions about how to play with mixed articulation patterns in section 1.2.

Harmonic Minor Scales Practice Log
Play all 12 harmonic minor scales from ♪ = 60 to ♪ = 220.

	60	80	100	120	140	160	180	200	220
C									
G									
D									
A									
E									
B									
F#/Gb									
Db									
Ab									
Eb									
Bb									
F									

2.3. PLAY ALL MODES OF ALL 12 HARMONIC MINOR SCALES (ONE OCTAVE ONLY)

C Harmonic Minor Modes

MODE NUMBER:	SCALE NAME:	SCALE RECIPE:
1st mode	Harmonic Minor	1 2 ♭3 4 5 ♭6 7 8
2nd mode	Locrian #6	1 ♭2 ♭3 4 ♭5 6 ♭7 8
3rd mode	Ionian Augmented	1 2 3 4 #5 6 7 8
4th mode	Romanian	1 2 ♭3 #4 5 6 ♭7 8
5th mode	Phrygian Dominant	1 ♭2 3 4 5 ♭6 ♭7 8
6th mode	Lydian #2	1 #2 3 #4 5 6 7 8
7th mode	Ultralocrian	1 ♭2 ♭3 ♭4 ♭5 ♭6 ♭♭7 8

Modes of the Harmonic Minor Scales Practice Log

Play all modes of all 12 harmonic minor scales from ♪ = 60 to ♪ = 220.

	60		80		100		120		140		160		180		200		220	
C	1	5	1	5	1	5	1	5	1	5	1	5	1	5	1	5	1	5
	2	6	2	6	2	6	2	6	2	6	2	6	2	6	2	6	2	6
	3	7	3	7	3	7	3	7	3	7	3	7	3	7	3	7	3	7
	4		4		4		4		4		4		4		4		4	
G	1	5	1	5	1	5	1	5	1	5	1	5	1	5	1	5	1	5
	2	6	2	6	2	6	2	6	2	6	2	6	2	6	2	6	2	6
	3	7	3	7	3	7	3	7	3	7	3	7	3	7	3	7	3	7
	4		4		4		4		4		4		4		4		4	
D	1	5	1	5	1	5	1	5	1	5	1	5	1	5	1	5	1	5
	2	6	2	6	2	6	2	6	2	6	2	6	2	6	2	6	2	6
	3	7	3	7	3	7	3	7	3	7	3	7	3	7	3	7	3	7
	4		4		4		4		4		4		4		4		4	
A	1	5	1	5	1	5	1	5	1	5	1	5	1	5	1	5	1	5
	2	6	2	6	2	6	2	6	2	6	2	6	2	6	2	6	2	6
	3	7	3	7	3	7	3	7	3	7	3	7	3	7	3	7	3	7
	4		4		4		4		4		4		4		4		4	
E	1	5	1	5	1	5	1	5	1	5	1	5	1	5	1	5	1	5
	2	6	2	6	2	6	2	6	2	6	2	6	2	6	2	6	2	6
	3	7	3	7	3	7	3	7	3	7	3	7	3	7	3	7	3	7
	4		4		4		4		4		4		4		4		4	
B	1	5	1	5	1	5	1	5	1	5	1	5	1	5	1	5	1	5
	2	6	2	6	2	6	2	6	2	6	2	6	2	6	2	6	2	6
	3	7	3	7	3	7	3	7	3	7	3	7	3	7	3	7	3	7
	4		4		4		4		4		4		4		4		4	
F#/G♭	1	5	1	5	1	5	1	5	1	5	1	5	1	5	1	5	1	5
	2	6	2	6	2	6	2	6	2	6	2	6	2	6	2	6	2	6
	3	7	3	7	3	7	3	7	3	7	3	7	3	7	3	7	3	7
	4		4		4		4		4		4		4		4		4	
D♭	1	5	1	5	1	5	1	5	1	5	1	5	1	5	1	5	1	5
	2	6	2	6	2	6	2	6	2	6	2	6	2	6	2	6	2	6
	3	7	3	7	3	7	3	7	3	7	3	7	3	7	3	7	3	7
	4		4		4		4		4		4		4		4		4	
A♭	1	5	1	5	1	5	1	5	1	5	1	5	1	5	1	5	1	5
	2	6	2	6	2	6	2	6	2	6	2	6	2	6	2	6	2	6
	3	7	3	7	3	7	3	7	3	7	3	7	3	7	3	7	3	7
	4		4		4		4		4		4		4		4		4	
E♭	1	5	1	5	1	5	1	5	1	5	1	5	1	5	1	5	1	5
	2	6	2	6	2	6	2	6	2	6	2	6	2	6	2	6	2	6
	3	7	3	7	3	7	3	7	3	7	3	7	3	7	3	7	3	7
	4		4		4		4		4		4		4		4		4	
B♭	1	5	1	5	1	5	1	5	1	5	1	5	1	5	1	5	1	5
	2	6	2	6	2	6	2	6	2	6	2	6	2	6	2	6	2	6
	3	7	3	7	3	7	3	7	3	7	3	7	3	7	3	7	3	7
	4		4		4		4		4		4		4		4		4	
F	1	5	1	5	1	5	1	5	1	5	1	5	1	5	1	5	1	5
	2	6	2	6	2	6	2	6	2	6	2	6	2	6	2	6	2	6
	3	7	3	7	3	7	3	7	3	7	3	7	3	7	3	7	3	7
	4		4		4		4		4		4		4		4		4	

2.4. PLAY ALL MINOR TRIAD ARPEGGIOS ON THE ENTIRE RANGE OF YOUR INSTRUMENT

Tip: Review the theory about minor triads (1, ♭3, 5) in the chapter 1.

C Minor Triad

Straight

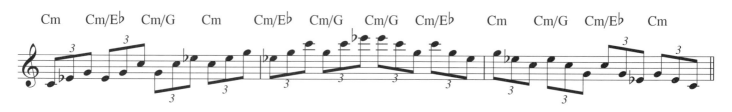

Broken in groups of three

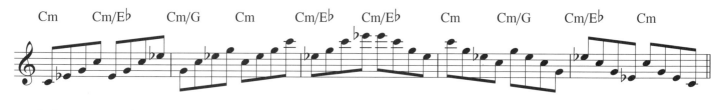

Broken in groups of four

Minor Triad Arpeggios Practice Log

Play all minor triad arpeggios (1, ♭3, 5) from ♪ = 60 to ♪ = 220.

	60	80	100	120	140	160	180	200	220
C									
G									
D									
A									
E									
B									
F#/G♭									
D♭									
A♭									
E♭									
B♭									
F									

2.5. CHAPTER 2 RESEARCH ASSIGNMENTS

The chapter assignments should be a part of your weekly practice routine. Each square (below) equals one hour spent doing research. Copy the template "Analytical Listening" in section 9.16. and use it for each player.

Watching (YouTube)

☐ ☐ ☐ ☐ Lester Young

☐ ☐ ☐ ☐ Oliver Nelson

☐ ☐ ☐ ☐ Wayne Shorter

☐ ☐ ☐ ☐ David Sanborn

☐ ☐ ☐ ☐ Greg Osby

Reading (Wikipedia, artist's website, saxophone websites, etc.)

☐ ☐ Lester Young

☐ ☐ Oliver Nelson

☐ ☐ Wayne Shorter

☐ ☐ David Sanborn

☐ ☐ Greg Osby

Listening (iTunes, public library, etc.)

☐ ☐ ☐ Lester Young

☐ ☐ ☐ Oliver Nelson

☐ ☐ ☐ Wayne Shorter

☐ ☐ ☐ David Sanborn

☐ ☐ ☐ Greg Osby

2.6. TEST: CHAPTER 2

Q1: What is the number formula of the harmonic minor scale?

A1:

Q2: What are the notes of E harmonic minor?

A2:

Q3: What are the notes of A♭ harmonic minor?

A3:

Q4: What are the notes of B harmonic minor?

A4:

Q5: What is the fourth mode of harmonic minor called?

A5:

Q6: What is the fifth mode of harmonic minor called?

A6:

Q7: What is the first mode of harmonic minor called?

A7:

Q8: What are the notes of the Dm triad?

A8:

Q9: What are the notes of the Fm/A♭ triad?

A9:

Q10: What are the notes of a Cm/G triad?

A10:

Do not continue with the next chapter before you have internalized everything from this chapter!

CHAPTER 3

3.1. THEORY: MELODIC MINOR SCALES

Like the major scales, the melodic minor scales are made up of eight notes. The difference is that in a melodic minor scale, the third note gets lowered by a half step.

Ex.1 Major scale

Ex. 2 Melodic minor scale

There are two different melodic minor scales: the classical melodic minor scale and the jazz melodic minor scale. The jazz melodic minor scale has a ♭3 when ascending and when descending. The classical melodic minor scale has a ♭3 when ascending, but when descending it gets a ♭3, ♭6, and a ♭7, like a natural minor scale. The melodic minor scales in this book will always be jazz melodic minor scales.

Recipe to get a melodic minor scale:
Take a major scale.
Lower the third note a half step by adding a flat or taking away a sharp.

D Major: D E F♯ G A B C♯ D
D Melodic Minor: D E F G A B C♯ D

Ex. 3 D melodic minor

3.2. PLAY ALL MAJOR, HARMONIC MINOR, AND MELODIC MINOR SCALES

Remember: Scales should always be played on the entire range of your instrument.

C Melodic Minor

Major, Harmonic Minor, and Melodic Minor Scales Practice Log

Play all major (1), harmonic minor (2), and melodic minor (3) scales from ♪ = 60 to ♪ = 220.

	60			80	100	120	140	160	180	200	220
C	1	2	3								
G											
D											
A											
E											
B											
F#/Gb											
Db											
Ab											
Eb											
Bb											
F											

3.3. PLAY ALL AUGMENTED (1-3-#5) AND DIMINISHED (1-♭3-♭5) TRIADS

Tip: You can review the theory about augmented and diminished triads in section 1.5.

C Augmented Triad

Straight

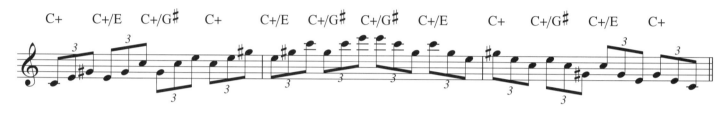

Broken in groups of three

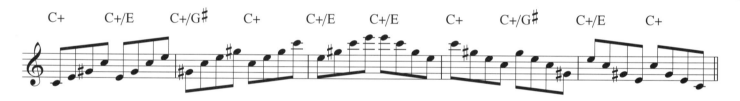

Broken in groups of four

Augmented Triads Practice Log

Play all augmented triads (1, 3, #5) from ♪ = 60 to ♪ = 220.

	60	80	100	120	140	160	180	200	220
C									
G									
D									
A									
E									
B									
F#/Gb									
Db									
Ab									
Eb									
Bb									
F									

C Diminished Triad

Straight (Go up to high Gb/F#, if you have a high F# key.)

Broken in groups of three (Go up to high Gb/F#, if you have a high F# key.)

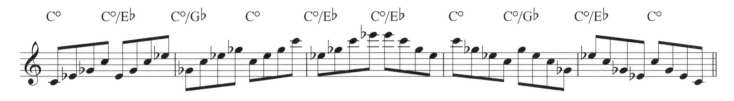

Broken in groups of four (Go up to high Gb/F#, if you have a high F# key.)

Tip: You can combine all 12 diminished triads in only three short scales. In each scale, you can find four diminished triads. The four diminished triads of the first line are:

(C, Eb, and Gb), (Eb, Gb/F#, and A), (F#, A, and C), and (A, C, and Eb).

Diminished Triads Practice Log

Play all diminished triads (1, ♭3, ♭5) from ♪ = 60 to ♪ = 220.

	60	80	100	120	140	160	180	200	220
C									
G									
D									
A									
E									
B									
F#/G♭									
D♭									
A♭									
E♭									
B♭									
F									

3.4. PLAY ALL MODES OF ALL 12 MELODIC MINOR SCALES

C Melodic Minor Modes

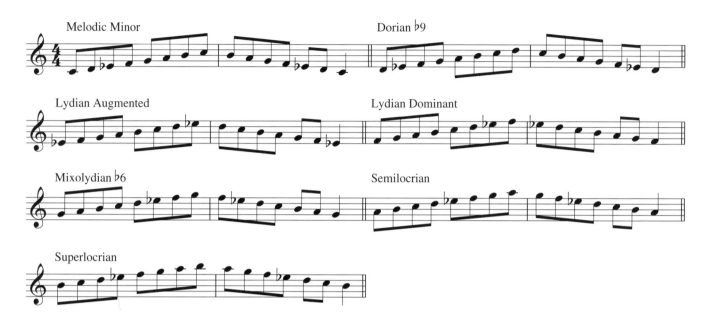

MODE NUMBER:	SCALE NAME:	SCALE RECIPE:
1st mode	Melodic minor	1 2 ♭3 4 5 6 7 8
2nd mode	Dorian ♭9	1 ♭2 ♭3 4 5 6 ♭7 8
3rd mode	Lydian Augmented	1 2 3 ♯4 ♯5 6 7 8
4th mode	Lydian Dominant	1 2 3 ♯4 5 6 ♭7 8
5th mode	Mixolydian ♭6	1 2 3 4 5 ♭6 ♭7 8
6th mode	Semilocrian	1 2 ♭3 4 ♭5 ♭6 ♭7 8
7th mode	Superlocrian	1 ♭2 ♭3 ♭4 ♭5 ♭6 ♭7 8

Modes of Melodic Minor Practice Log

Play all modes of all 12 melodic minor scales from ♪ = 60 to ♪ = 220.

	60		80		100		120		140		160		180		200		220	
C	1	5	1	5	1	5	1	5	1	5	1	5	1	5	1	5	1	5
	2	6	2	6	2	6	2	6	2	6	2	6	2	6	2	6	2	6
	3	7	3	7	3	7	3	7	3	7	3	7	3	7	3	7	3	7
	4		4		4		4		4		4		4		4		4	
G	1	5	1	5	1	5	1	5	1	5	1	5	1	5	1	5	1	5
	2	6	2	6	2	6	2	6	2	6	2	6	2	6	2	6	2	6
	3	7	3	7	3	7	3	7	3	7	3	7	3	7	3	7	3	7
	4		4		4		4		4		4		4		4		4	
D	1	5	1	5	1	5	1	5	1	5	1	5	1	5	1	5	1	5
	2	6	2	6	2	6	2	6	2	6	2	6	2	6	2	6	2	6
	3	7	3	7	3	7	3	7	3	7	3	7	3	7	3	7	3	7
	4		4		4		4		4		4		4		4		4	
A	1	5	1	5	1	5	1	5	1	5	1	5	1	5	1	5	1	5
	2	6	2	6	2	6	2	6	2	6	2	6	2	6	2	6	2	6
	3	7	3	7	3	7	3	7	3	7	3	7	3	7	3	7	3	7
	4		4		4		4		4		4		4		4		4	
E	1	5	1	5	1	5	1	5	1	5	1	5	1	5	1	5	1	5
	2	6	2	6	2	6	2	6	2	6	2	6	2	6	2	6	2	6
	3	7	3	7	3	7	3	7	3	7	3	7	3	7	3	7	3	7
	4		4		4		4		4		4		4		4		4	
B	1	5	1	5	1	5	1	5	1	5	1	5	1	5	1	5	1	5
	2	6	2	6	2	6	2	6	2	6	2	6	2	6	2	6	2	6
	3	7	3	7	3	7	3	7	3	7	3	7	3	7	3	7	3	7
	4		4		4		4		4		4		4		4		4	
F#/Gb	1	5	1	5	1	5	1	5	1	5	1	5	1	5	1	5	1	5
	2	6	2	6	2	6	2	6	2	6	2	6	2	6	2	6	2	6
	3	7	3	7	3	7	3	7	3	7	3	7	3	7	3	7	3	7
	4		4		4		4		4		4		4		4		4	
Db	1	5	1	5	1	5	1	5	1	5	1	5	1	5	1	5	1	5
	2	6	2	6	2	6	2	6	2	6	2	6	2	6	2	6	2	6
	3	7	3	7	3	7	3	7	3	7	3	7	3	7	3	7	3	7
	4		4		4		4		4		4		4		4		4	
Ab	1	5	1	5	1	5	1	5	1	5	1	5	1	5	1	5	1	5
	2	6	2	6	2	6	2	6	2	6	2	6	2	6	2	6	2	6
	3	7	3	7	3	7	3	7	3	7	3	7	3	7	3	7	3	7
	4		4		4		4		4		4		4		4		4	
Eb	1	5	1	5	1	5	1	5	1	5	1	5	1	5	1	5	1	5
	2	6	2	6	2	6	2	6	2	6	2	6	2	6	2	6	2	6
	3	7	3	7	3	7	3	7	3	7	3	7	3	7	3	7	3	7
	4		4		4		4		4		4		4		4		4	
Bb	1	5	1	5	1	5	1	5	1	5	1	5	1	5	1	5	1	5
	2	6	2	6	2	6	2	6	2	6	2	6	2	6	2	6	2	6
	3	7	3	7	3	7	3	7	3	7	3	7	3	7	3	7	3	7
	4		4		4		4		4		4		4		4		4	
F	1	5	1	5	1	5	1	5	1	5	1	5	1	5	1	5	1	5
	2	6	2	6	2	6	2	6	2	6	2	6	2	6	2	6	2	6
	3	7	3	7	3	7	3	7	3	7	3	7	3	7	3	7	3	7
	4		4		4		4		4		4		4		4		4	

3.5 THEORY: DIATONIC TRIADS

Ex. 1 Diatonic triads of C major

All the triads above are diatonic to C major because every note you see in Ex. 1 belongs to the C major scale.

Recipe for the diatonic triads of a scale:

1. Take a scale.

2. Place two notes on each scale note using intervals (vertical space) of thirds.

3. Analyze the resulting thirds and label them.

Ex. 2 Diatonic triads of G harmonic minor

Take a scale (G harmonic minor): G A B♭ C D E♭ F♯ G

Place two notes on each scale note using intervals of thirds.

Analyze the resulting thirds and label them.

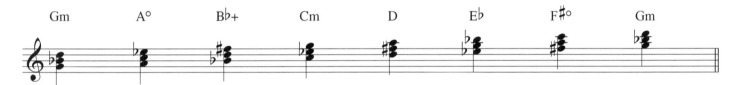

G harmonic minor has a B♭, an E♭, and an F♯. Therefore, all notes in the above example are diatonic to G harmonic minor.

Tip: Play all triads above on a piano and internalize their sound.

3.6. PLAY ALL DIATONIC TRIADS OF THE MAJOR, HARMONIC MINOR, AND MELODIC MINOR KEYS

Listen carefully for the quality/flavor of the different triads.

C Major Diatonic Triads – All Ascending

C Major Diatonic Triads – Ascending & Descending

C Melodic Minor Diatonic Triads – All Ascending

C Melodic Minor Diatonic Triads – Ascending & Descending

C Harmonic Minor Diatonic Triads – All Ascending

C Harmonic Minor Diatonic Triads – Ascending & Descending

Diatonic Triads Practice Log

Play all diatonic triads of the major (1), harmonic minor (2), and melodic minor (3) keys from ♪ = 60 to ♪ = 220.

	60	80	100	120	140	160	180	200	220
C	1 2 3								
G									
D									
A									
E									
B									
F#/Gb									
Db									
Ab									
Eb									
Bb									
F									

3.7. PLAY ALL MAJOR, HARMONIC MINOR, AND MELODIC MINOR SCALES IN DIATONIC THIRDS

C Major Scale in Diatonic Thirds

C Melodic Minor Scale in Diatonic Thirds

C Harmonic Minor Scale in Diatonic Thirds

Diatonic Thirds Practice Log

Play all major (1), harmonic minor (2), and melodic minor (3) scales in diatonic thirds from ♪ = 60 to ♪ = 220.

	60			80			100			120			140			160			180			200			220		
C	1	2	3																								
G																											
D																											
A																											
E																											
B																											
F♯/G♭																											
D♭																											
A♭																											
E♭																											
B♭																											
F																											

3.8. CHAPTER 3 RESEARCH ASSIGNMENTS

The chapter assignments should be a part of your weekly practice routine. Each square (below) equals one hour spent doing research. Copy the template "Analytical Listening" in section 9.16. and use it for each player.

Watching (YouTube)

☐ ☐ ☐ ☐ Benny Carter

☐ ☐ ☐ ☐ Earl Bostic

☐ ☐ ☐ ☐ Michael Brecker

☐ ☐ ☐ ☐ Phil Woods

☐ ☐ ☐ ☐ Joe Lovano

Reading (Wikipedia, artist's website, saxophone websites, etc.)

☐ ☐ Benny Carter

☐ ☐ Earl Bostic

☐ ☐ Michael Brecker

☐ ☐ Phil Woods

☐ ☐ Joe Lovano

Listening (iTunes, public library, etc.)

☐ ☐ ☐ Benny Carter

☐ ☐ ☐ Earl Bostic

☐ ☐ ☐ Michael Brecker

☐ ☐ ☐ Phil Woods

☐ ☐ ☐ Joe Lovano

3.9. TEST: CHAPTER 3

Q1: What is the number formula of the melodic minor scale?

A1:

Q2: What are the notes of E melodic minor?

A2:

Q3: What are the notes of D♭ melodic minor?

A3:

Q4: What are the notes of F♯ melodic minor?

A4:

Q5: What are the notes of the C augmented triad?

A5:

Q6: What are the notes of the B♭ diminished triad?

A6:

Q7: What are the notes of the A augmented triad?

A7:

Q8: What are the notes of the G diminished triad?

A8:

Q9: What is the second mode of melodic minor called?

A9:

Q10: What is the third mode of melodic minor called?

A10:

Do not continue with the next chapter before you have internalized everything from this chapter!

CHAPTER 4

4.1. PLAY ALL MAJOR, HARMONIC, AND MELODIC MINOR SCALES IN DIATONIC FOURTHS

C Major Scale in Diatonic Fourths

C Melodic Minor Scale in Diatonic Fourths

C Harmonic Minor Scale in Diatonic Fourths

Diatonic Fourths Practice Log

Play all major (1), harmonic minor (2), and melodic minor (3) scales in diatonic fourths from ♪ = 60 to ♪ = 220.

	60			80			100			120			140			160			180			200			220		
C	1	2	3																								
G																											
D																											
A																											
E																											
B																											
F#/G♭																											
D♭																											
A♭																											
E♭																											
B♭																											
F																											

4.2. THEORY: 7TH CHORDS AND 6TH CHORDS

A 7th chord is a triad with another third added to the top note. Or, four notes in intervals of thirds on top of each other. The top note is a seventh above the bottom note.

A 6th chord is a triad with a second added to the top note. The top note is a sixth above the bottom note.

There are seven different 7th chords (A) and two different 6th chords (B):

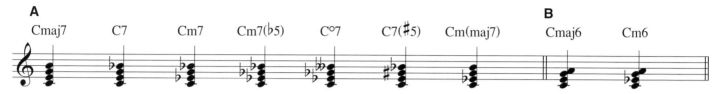

CHORD SYMBOL	CHORD NAME	CHORD RECIPE
Cmaj7	Major seventh chord	1 3 5 7
C7	Dominant seventh chord	1 3 5 ♭7
Cm7	Minor seventh chord	1 ♭3 5 ♭7
Cm7(♭5)	Minor seventh (♭5) chord	1 ♭3 ♭5 ♭7
C°7	Diminished seventh chord	1 ♭3 ♭5 ♭♭7
C7(♯5)	Augmented seventh chord	1 3 ♯5 ♭7
Cm(maj7)	Minor major seventh chord	1 ♭3 5 7
Cmaj6	Major sixth chord	1 3 5 6
Cm6	Minor sixth chord	1 ♭3 5 6

Diatonic 7th chords of a major scale:

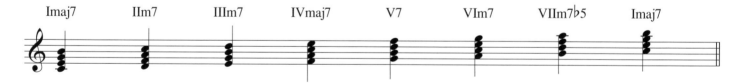

All notes in the example above are diatonic to (part of) the C major scale. Therefore, all 7th chords in the example above are diatonic to the C major scale. The Roman numerals indicate that in any major scale, the first diatonic 7th chord will be a major 7th chord, the second diatonic 7th chord will be a minor 7th chord, etc.

Example:
The second note of the D major scale is E. The quality of the second diatonic 7th chord of any major scale is a minor 7th chord. Therefore, the second diatonic 7th chord of the D major scale is Em7.

As always, listen to how these chords sound on a piano.

4.3. PLAY ALL 7TH CHORDS AND 6TH CHORDS ARPEGGIOS

Play all major 7th, dominant 7th, minor 7th, minor 7th (♭5), diminished 7th, augmented 7th, major 6th, and minor 6th chords, using different progressions/cycles.

The progression for the 7th chord examples is moving up in whole steps. Be sure to practice the 7th chords in all progressions/cycles. Use section 9.6. "Regular Progressions Worksheet" in the third part of this book as a guide.

Practice the 7th chords exercises on the entire range of your instrument.

Major Seventh Chords

Dominant Seventh Chords

Minor Seventh Chords

Minor Seventh (♭5) Chords

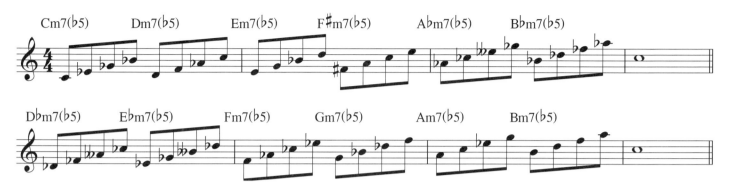

Diminished Seventh Chords

Augmented Seventh Chords

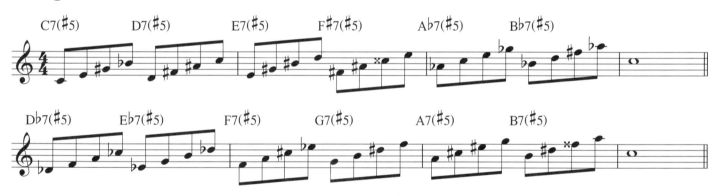

Major Sixth Chords

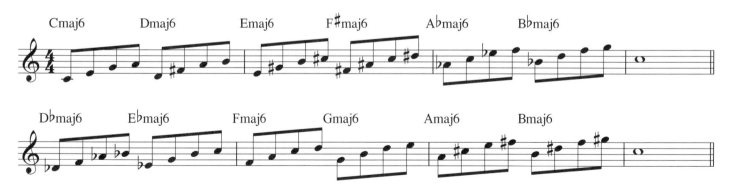

Minor Sixth Chords

7th Chords and 6th Chords Arpeggios Practice Log

Play all major 7th, dominant 7th, minor 7th, minor 7th (♭5), diminished 7th, augmented 7th, major 6th, and minor 6th chords, using different progressions/cycles from ♪ = 60 to ♪ = 220.

	60	80	100	120	140	160	180	200	220
Maj7 (1, 3, 5, 7)									
Dom7 (1, 3, 5, ♭7)									
Min7 (1, ♭3, 5, ♭7)									
Min7(♭5) (1, ♭3, ♭5, ♭7)									
Dim7 (1, ♭3, ♭5, ♭♭7)									
Aug7 (1, 3, ♯5, ♭7)									
Maj6 (1, 3, 5, 6)									
Min6 (1, ♭3, 5, 6)									

4.4. PLAY ALL DIATONIC 7TH CHORDS OF ALL MAJOR, HARMONIC, AND MELODIC MINOR KEYS

C Major Diatonic Seventh Chords – All Ascending

C Major Diatonic Seventh Chords – Ascending & Descending

C Melodic Minor Diatonic Secenth Chords – All Ascending

C Melodic Minor Diatonic Seventh Chords – Ascending & Descending

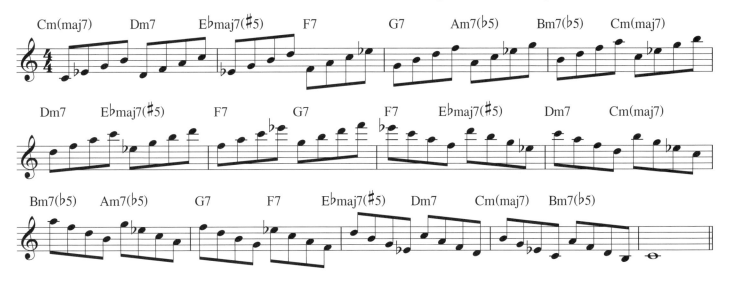

C Harmonic Minor Diatonic Seventh Chords – All Ascending

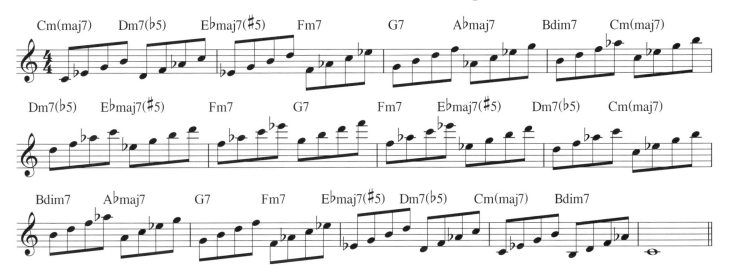

C Harmonic Minor Diatonic Seventh Chords – Ascending & Descending

Diatonic 7th Chords Practice Log

Play all diatonic 7th chords of all major (1), harmonic minor (2), and melodic minor (3) keys ♪ = 60 to ♪ = 220.

	60			80			100			120			140			160			180			200			220		
C	1	2	3																								
G																											
D																											
A																											
E																											
B																											
F#/G♭																											
D♭																											
A♭																											
E♭																											
B♭																											
F																											

4.5. THEORY: CHROMATIC SCALE

The chromatic scale has 12 different notes (that's all available notes). The structure of a chromatic scale is:

$$H-H-H-H-H-H-H-H-H-H-H-H$$

There is a lack of a clear beginning and end in the chromatic scale due to this very regular and even structure.
    Ex. 1 shows a chromatic scale starting and ending on C.

Ex. 1

There is only one chromatic scale but you can start and end it on different notes!

4.6. PLAY THE CHROMATIC SCALE ON THE ENTIRE RANGE OF YOUR INSTRUMENT

The chromatic scale is, besides the major scales, probably the most important scale. You want to master it at a very fast speed without sacrificing any accuracy. Note that the chromatic scale has no real sense of a beginning or an end.

Chromatic Scale Practice Log
Play the chromatic scale on the entire range of your instrument from ♪ = 60 to ♪ = 220.

60	80	100	120	140	160	180	200	220

4.7. CHAPTER 4 RESEARCH ASSIGNMENTS

The chapter assignments should be a part of your weekly practice routine. Each square (below) equals one hour spent doing research. Copy the template "Analytical Listening" in section 9.16. and use it for each player.

Watching (YouTube)

☐ ☐ ☐ ☐ Dexter Gordon

☐ ☐ ☐ ☐ Paul Desmond

☐ ☐ ☐ ☐ Eric Dolphy

☐ ☐ ☐ ☐ Maceo Parker

☐ ☐ ☐ ☐ Jerry Bergonzi

Reading (Wikipedia, artist's website, saxophone websites, etc.)

☐ ☐ Dexter Gordon

☐ ☐ Paul Desmond

☐ ☐ Eric Dolphy

☐ ☐ Maceo Parker

☐ ☐ Jerry Bergonzi

Listening (iTunes, public library, etc.)

☐ ☐ ☐ Dexter Gordon

☐ ☐ ☐ Paul Desmond

☐ ☐ ☐ Eric Dolphy

☐ ☐ ☐ Maceo Parker

☐ ☐ ☐ Jerry Bergonzi

4.8. TEST: CHAPTER 4

Q1: What is the whole/half step structure of a chromatic scale?

A1:

Q2: What are the notes of the E♭maj7 chord?

A2:

Q3: What are the notes of the F♯7 chord?

A3:

Q4: What are the notes of the B♭m7 chord?

A4:

Q5: What are the notes of the Gm7(♭5) chord?

A5:

Q6: What are the notes of the D°7 chord?

A6:

Q7: What are the notes of the F7(♯5) chord?

A7:

Q8: What are the notes of the A♭m(maj7) chord?

A8:

Q9: What are the notes of the Cmaj6 chord?

A9:

Q10: What are the notes of the Em6 chord?

A10:

Do not continue with the next chapter before you have internalized everything from this chapter!

CHAPTER 5

5.1. PLAY ALL MAJOR, HARMONIC, AND MELODIC MINOR SCALES IN DIATONIC FIFTHS

C Major Scale in Diatonic Fifths

C Melodic Minor Scale in Diatonic Fifths

C Harmonic Minor Scale in Diatonic Fifths

Diatonic Fifths Practice Log

Play all major (1), harmonic minor (2), and melodic minor (3) scales in diatonic fifths from ♪ = 60 to ♪ = 220.

	60			80			100			120			140			160			180			200			220		
C	1	2	3																								
G																											
D																											
A																											
E																											
B																											
F♯/G♭																											
D♭																											
A♭																											
E♭																											
B♭																											
F																											

5.2. THEORY: 7TH CHORDS WITH TENSIONS

Remember how we took triads and stacked another note on top of them to get 7th chords? Well, can we continue stacking notes in the same way? Sure we can!

Example 1 shows all notes of a major scale stacked on top of each other using intervals (vertical space) of thirds. If you would continue stacking thirds beyond the notes in example 1 you would start to repeat notes.

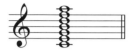

Ex. 1. Chord tones vs. tensions

The first four notes from the bottom up (1, 3, 5, 7) are called chord tones. The three top notes (9, 11, 13) are called tensions. When tensions occur in different octaves we still call them 9, 11, and 13. Tensions can be flat or sharp just like chord tones (i.e. ♭9, ♯11, ♭13).

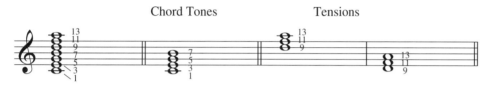

Ex. 2. 7th chords with tensions

Please check out section 9.14. "Alternate chord symbols" to get more information about how people write the same chord symbols in different ways.

The following are the 7th chords with tensions that we are going to use in this book.

Ninth chords

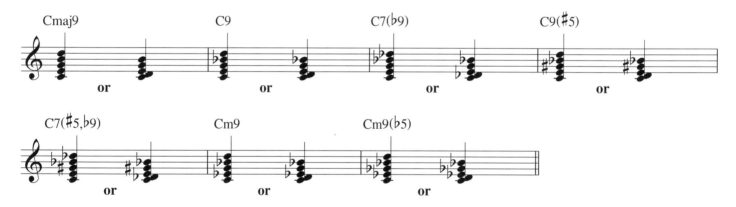

CHORD SYMBOL	CHORD NAME	CHORD RECIPE				
Cmaj9	Major ninth chord	1	3	5	7	9
C9	Dominant ninth chord	1	3	5	♭7	9
C7(♭9)	Dominant (♭9) chord	1	3	5	♭7	♭9
C9(#5)	Augmented ninth chord	1	3	#5	♭7	9
C7(#5, ♭9)	Augmented dominant (♭9) chord	1	3	#5	♭7	♭9
Cm9	Minor ninth chord	1	♭3	5	♭7	9
Cm9(♭5)	Minor ninth (♭5) chord	1	♭3	♭5	♭7	9

Observation: Having a tension nine implies that there is a seventh (chord tone) in the chord.

Eleventh chords (We will cover these more in Chapter 6.)

CHORD SYMBOL	CHORD NAME	CHORD RECIPE					
Cmaj9(#11)	Major ninth (#11) chord	1	3	5	7	9	#11
C11	Dominant eleventh chord	1	3	5	♭7	9	11
C9(#11)	Dominant ninth (#11) chord	1	3	5	♭7	9	#11
C9(#5, #11)	Dominant ninth (#5, #11) chord	1	3	#5	♭7	9	#11
Cm11	Minor eleventh chord	1	♭3	5	♭7	9	11
Cm11(♭5)	Minor eleventh (♭5) chord	1	♭3	♭5	♭7	9	11

Observation: Having a tension eleven implies that there is a seventh and a ninth in the chord.

Thirteenth chords (We will cover these more in Chapter 7.)

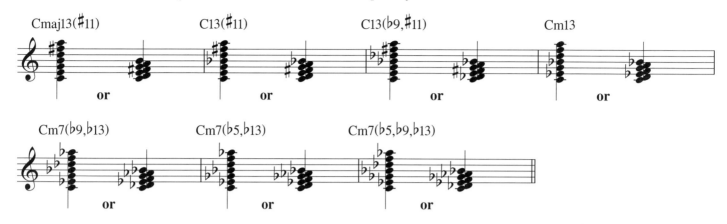

CHORD SYMBOL	CHORD NAME		CHORD RECIPE						
Cmaj13(#11)	Major thirteenth (#11) chord		1	3	5	7	9	#11	13
C13(#11)	Dominant thirteenth (#11) chord		1	3	5	♭7	9	#11	13
C13(♭9, #11)	Dominant thirteenth (♭9, #11) chord		1	3	5	♭7	♭9	#11	13
Cm13	Minor thirteenth chord		1	♭3	5	♭7	9	11	13
Cm7(♭9, ♭13)	Minor seventh (♭9, ♭13) chord		1	♭3	5	♭7	♭9	11	♭13
Cm7(♭5, ♭13)	Minor seventh (♭5, ♭13) chord		1	♭3	♭5	♭7	9	11	♭13
Cm7(♭5, ♭9, ♭13)	Minor seventh (♭5, ♭9, ♭13) chord		1	♭3	♭5	♭7	♭9	11	♭13

Observation: Having a tension thirteen implies that there is a seventh, a ninth, and an eleventh in the chord.

5.3. PLAY ALL 9TH CHORDS ARPEGGIOS

Play all major 9th, dominant 9th, dominant (♭9), minor 9th, augmented 9th, augmented dominant (♭9), and minor 9th (♭5) chords, using different progressions/cycles.

The progression for the 9th chord examples is moving up in whole steps. Be sure to practice the 9th chords in all progressions/cycles. Remember to use section 9.6. "Regular Progressions Worksheet" in the third part of this book as a guide.

Practice the 9th chords exercises on the entire range of your instrument.

The 9th chord arpeggios are presented as eighth note quintuplets. This is that this allows a clean understandable presentation. Feel free to practice the arpeggios playing eighth notes instead of eighth note quintuplets.

Major Ninth Chords

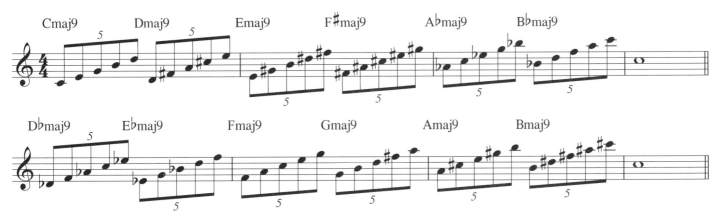

Dominant Ninth Chords

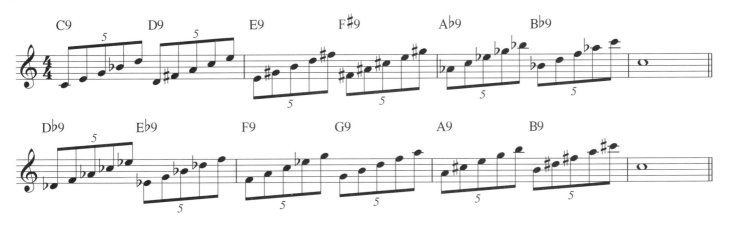

Dominant (♭9) Chords

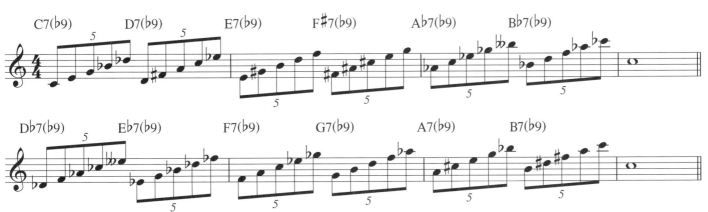

Augmented Ninth Chords

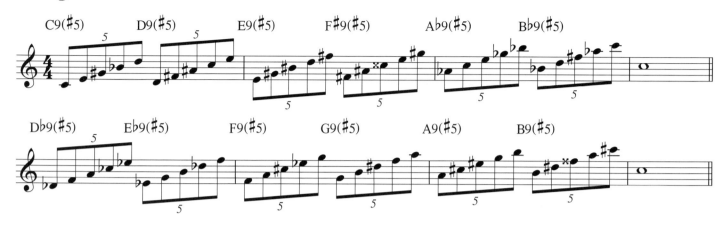

Augmented Dominant (♭9) Chords

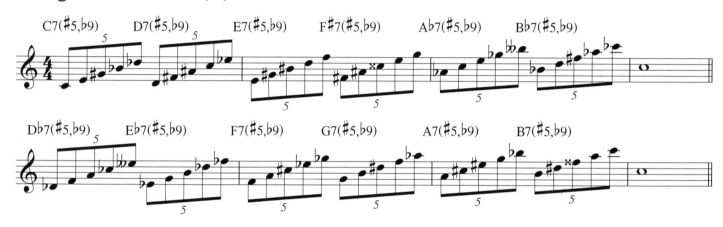

Minor Ninth Chords

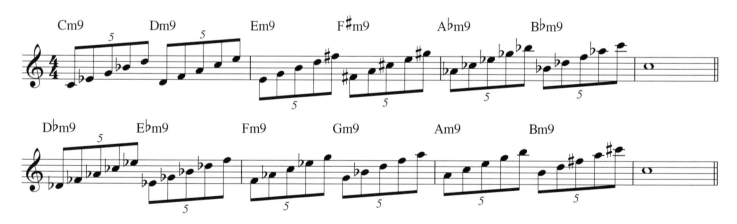

Minor Ninth (♭5) Chords

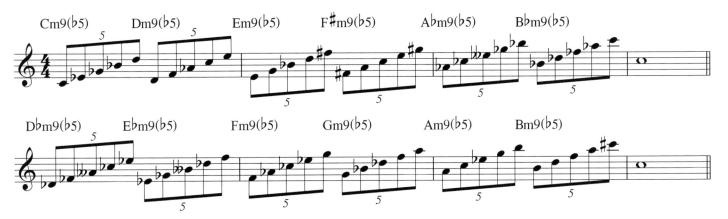

Ninth Chords Arpeggios Practice Log

Play all major 9th, dominant 9th, dominant (♭9), minor 9th, augmented 9th, augmented dominant (♭9), and minor 9th (♭5) chords, using different progressions/cycles from ♪ = 60 to ♪ = 220.

	60	80	100	120	140	160	180	200	220
Maj9 (1, 3, 5, 7, 9)									
Dom9 (1, 3, 5, ♭7, 9)									
Dom7(♭9) (1, 3, 5, ♭7, ♭9)									
Min9 (1, ♭3, 5, ♭7, 9)									
Aug9 (1, 3, #5, ♭7, 9)									
Aug7(♭9) (1, 3, #5, ♭7, b9)									
Min9(♭5) (1, ♭3, 5, ♭7, ♭9)									

5.4. PLAY ALL DIATONIC 9TH CHORDS OF THE MAJOR, HARMONIC, AND MELODIC MINOR KEYS

C Major Diatonic Ninth Chords – All Ascending

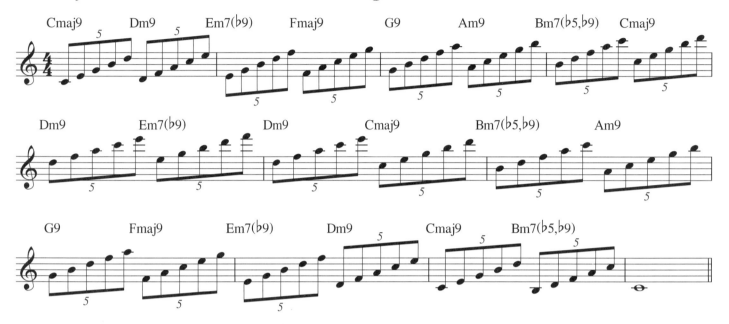

C Major Diatonic Ninth Chords – Ascending & Descending

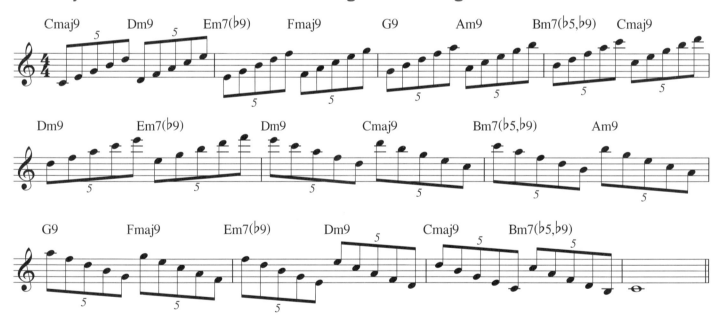

C Melodic Minor Diatonic Ninth Chords – All Ascending

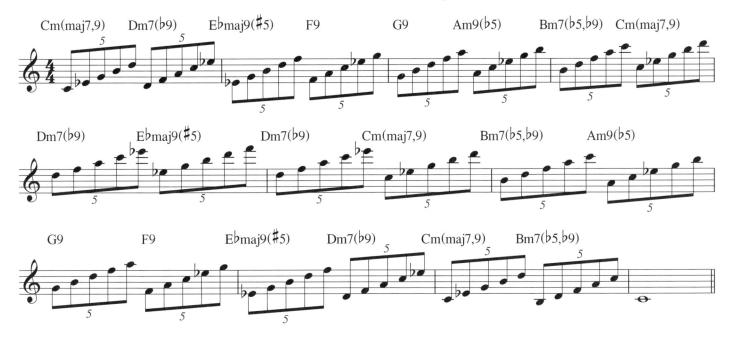

C Melodic Minor Diatonic Ninth Chords – Ascending & Descending

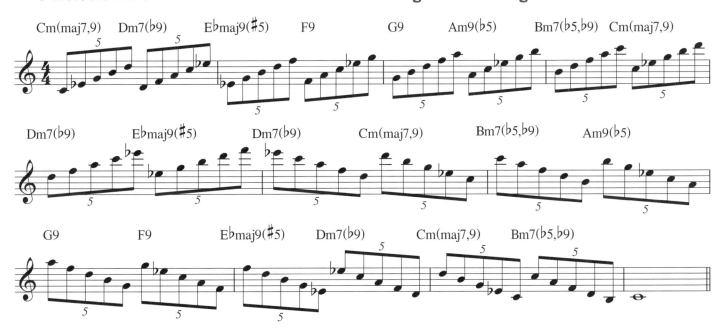

C Harmonic Minor Diatonic Ninth Chords – All Ascending

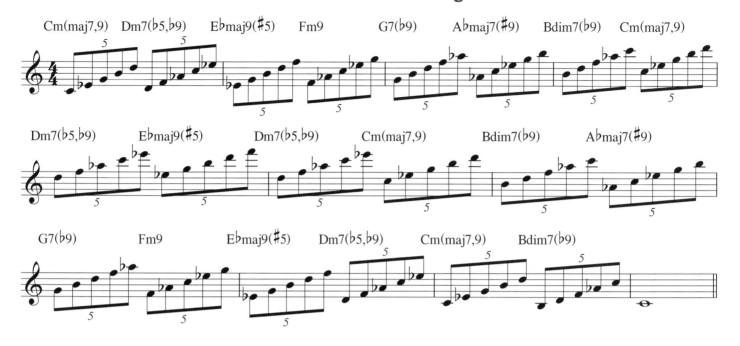

C Harmonic Minor Diatonic Ninth Chords – Ascending & Descending

Diatonic Ninth Chords Practice Log

Play all diatonic 9th chords of the major (1), harmonic minor (2), and melodic minor (3) keys from ♪ = 60 to ♪ = 220.

	60	80	100	120	140	160	180	200	220
C	1 2 3								
G									
D									
A									
E									
B									
F#/Gb									
Db									
Ab									
Eb									
Bb									
F									

5.5. THEORY: PENTATONIC SCALES

A pentatonic scale is made up of five notes (penta is Greek for five). In this book, we will focus on major pentatonic scales and minor pentatonic scales only.

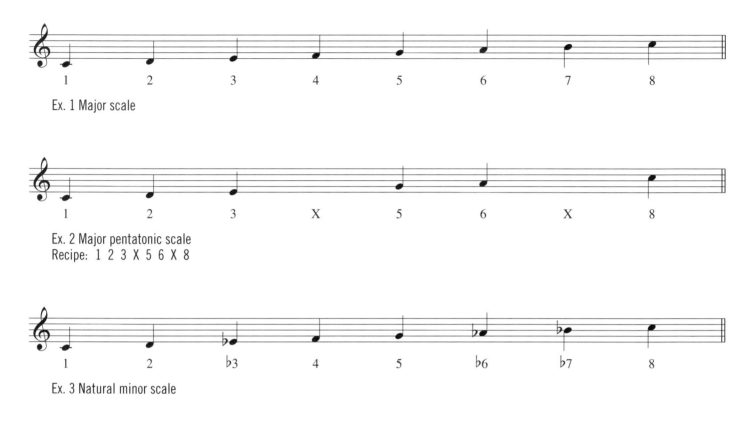

Ex. 1 Major scale

Ex. 2 Major pentatonic scale
Recipe: 1 2 3 X 5 6 X 8

Ex. 3 Natural minor scale

Ex. 4 Minor pentatonic scale
Recipe: 1 X ♭3 4 5 X ♭7 8

5.6. PLAY ALL MAJOR AND MINOR PENTATONIC SCALES

Major Pentatonic

C Pentatonic

Minor Pentatonic

C Minor Pentatonic

Major and Minor Pentatonic Scales Practice Log

Play all major pentatonic (1) and minor pentatonic (2) scales from ♪ = 60 to ♪ = 220.

	60		80		100		120		140		160		180		200		220	
C	1	2																
G																		
D																		
A																		
E																		
B																		
F#/Gb																		
Db																		
Ab																		
Eb																		
Bb																		
F																		

5.7. CHAPTER 5 RESEARCH ASSIGNMENTS

The chapter assignments should be a part of your weekly practice routine. Each square (below) equals one hour spent doing research. Copy the template "Analytical Listening" in section 9.16. and use it for each player.

Watching (YouTube)

☐ ☐ ☐ ☐   Sonny Stitt

☐ ☐ ☐ ☐   Gerry Mulligan

☐ ☐ ☐ ☐   Sonny Rollins

☐ ☐ ☐ ☐   Dave Liebman

☐ ☐ ☐ ☐   Branford Marsalis

Reading (Wikipedia, artist's website, saxophone websites, etc.)

☐ ☐   Sonny Stitt

☐ ☐   Gerry Mulligan

☐ ☐   Sonny Rollins

☐ ☐   Dave Liebman

☐ ☐   Branford Marsalis

Listening (iTunes, public library, etc.)

☐ ☐ ☐   Sonny Stitt

☐ ☐ ☐   Gerry Mulligan

☐ ☐ ☐   Sonny Rollins

☐ ☐ ☐   Dave Liebman

☐ ☐ ☐   Branford Marsalis

5.8. TEST: CHAPTER 5

Q1: What are the notes of the G♭ major pentatonic scale?

A1:

Q2: What are the notes of the B minor pentatonic scale?

A2:

Q3: What does a tension nine imply?

A3:

Q4: What are the notes of the Cmaj9 chord?

A4:

Q5: What are the notes of the E♭9 chord?

A5:

Q6: What are the notes of the A7(♭9) chord?

A6:

Q7: What are the notes of the F9(♯5) chord?

A7:

Q8: What are the notes of the B♭7(♯5, ♭9) chord?

A8:

Q9: What are the notes of the Gm9 chord?

A9:

Q10: What are the notes of the D♭m9(♭5) chord?

A10:

Do not continue with the next chapter before you have internalized everything from this chapter!

CHAPTER 6

PLAY ALL MAJOR, HARMONIC, AND MELODIC MINOR SCALES IN DIATONIC SIXTHS

C Major Scale in Diatonic Sixths

C Melodic Minor Scale in Diatonic Sixths

C Harmonic Minor Scale in Diatonic Sixths

Diatonic Sixths Practice Log

Play all major (1), harmonic (2), and melodic minor (3) in diatonic sixths from ♪ = 60 to ♪ = 220.

	60	80	100	120	140	160	180	200	220
C	1　2　3								
G									
D									
A									
E									
B									
F#/Gb									
Db									
Ab									
Eb									
Bb									
F									

6.2. PLAY ALL DIATONIC 11TH CHORDS OF THE MAJOR, HARMONIC, AND MELODIC MINOR KEYS

The 11th chords are presented as eighth note sextuplets. This allows for a clean and understandable presentation. Feel free to practice the 11th chords playing eighth notes instead of eight note sextuplets.

C Major Diatonic Eleventh Chords – All Ascending

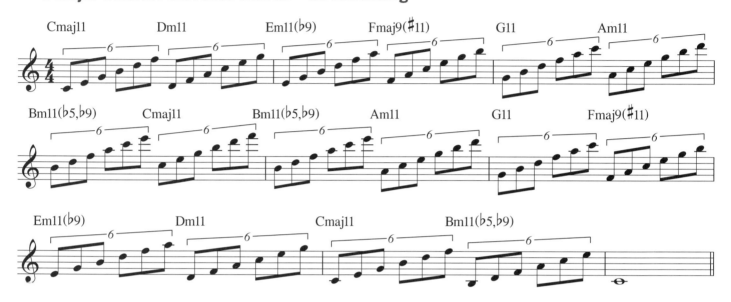

C Major Diatonic Eleventh Chords – Ascending & Descending

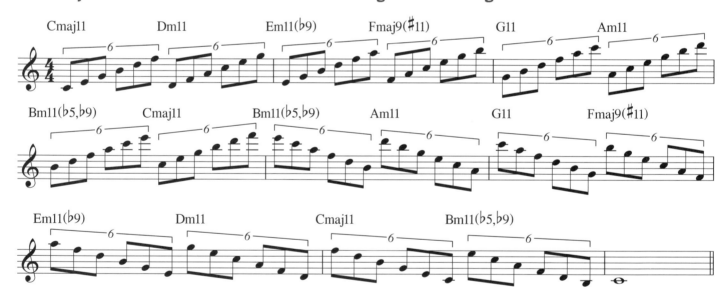

C Melodic Minor Diatonic Eleventh Chords – All Ascending

C Melodic Minor Diatonic Eleventh Chords – Ascending & Descending

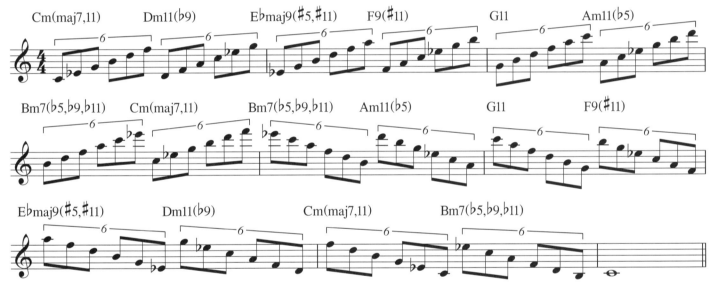

C Harmonic Minor Diatonic Eleventh Chords – All Ascending

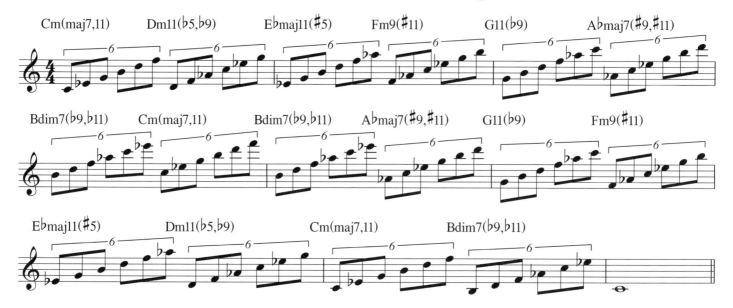

C Harmonic Minor Diatonic Eleventh Chords – Ascending & Descending

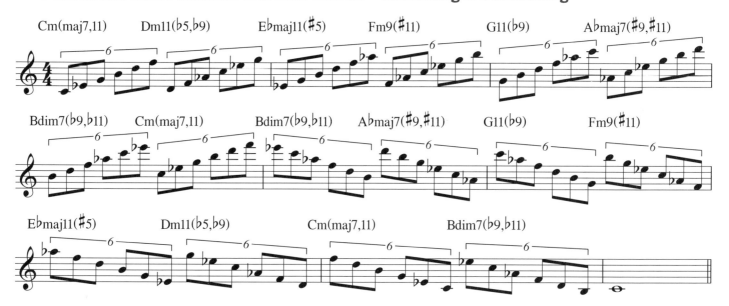

Diatonic Eleventh Chords Practice Log

Play all diatonic 11th chords of the major (1), harmonic minor (2), and melodic minor (3) keys from ♪ = 60 to ♪ = 220.

	60			80	100	120	140	160	180	200	220
C	1	2	3								
G											
D											
A											
E											
B											
F#/Gb											
Db											
Ab											
Eb											
Bb											
F											

6.3. PLAY THE 11TH CHORDS ARPEGGIOS

Play all major 9th (#11), dominant 11th, dominant 9th (#11), dominant 9th (#5, #11), minor 11th, and minor 11th (♭5) chords, using different progressions/cycles.

   The progression for the 11th chord examples is moving up in whole steps. Be sure to practice the 11th chords in all progressions/cycles. Remember to use section 9.6. "Regular Progressions Worksheet" in the third part of this book as a guide.

   Practice the 11th chord exercises on the entire range of your instrument.

Major Ninth (#11) Chords

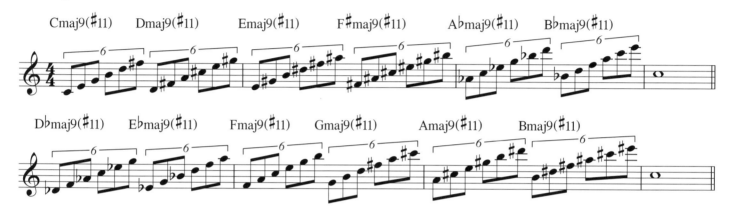

Dominant Eleventh Chords

Dominant Ninth (#11) Chords

Major Ninth (♯5, ♯11) Chords

Minor Eleventh Chords

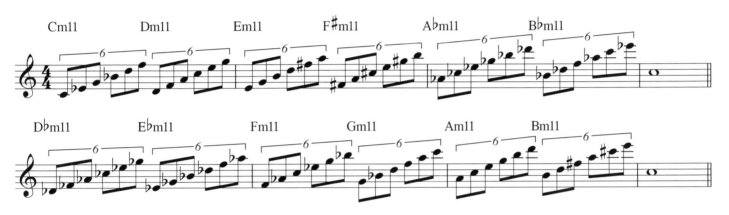

Minor Eleventh (♭5) Chords

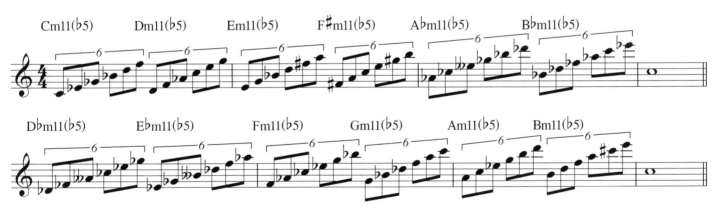

Eleventh Chords Arpeggios Practice Log

Play all major 9th (#11), dominant 11th, dominant 9th (#11), dominant 9th (#5, #11), minor 11th, and minor 11th (♭5) chords, using different progressions/cycles from ♪ = 60 to ♪ = 220.

	60	80	100	120	140	160	180	200	220
Maj9(#11) (1, 3, 5, 7, 9, #11)									
Dom11 (1, 3, 5, ♭7, 9, 11)									
Dom9(#11) (1, 3, 5, ♭7, 9, #11)									
Dom9(#5, #11) (1, 3, #5, ♭7, 9, #11)			·						
Min11 (1, ♭3, 5, ♭7, 9, 11)									
Min11(♭5) (1, ♭3, ♭5, ♭7, 9, 11)									

6.4. SIGHT-TRANSPOSE FROM CONCERT PITCH TO E♭ (FOR ALTO AND BARITONE PLAYERS) OR FROM CONCERT PITCH TO B♭ (FOR TENOR AND SOPRANO PLAYERS)

Being able to sightread fluently from concert parts to the key of your saxophone is a great skill to have. Here are the intervals of transposition:

* Baritone players: to read concert parts written in bass clef, replace the bass clef with a treble clef (do not move the notes up or down). Then add three sharps (or remove three flats) from the key signature.

Tip: Don't hesitate to do octave adjustments (play something an octave higher or lower). Start practicing sight-transposition with very easy music at a slow tempo. Do not get discouraged as this will take some time.

Sight-transposing simple music, such as your first saxophone book, is a great place to start!

6.5. THEORY: BLUES SCALES

A blues scale is made up of six notes. Let's compare it to a major scale:

1   2   3   4   5   6   7   8

Ex. 1 Major scale

1   X   ♭3   4   ♭5   5   X   ♭7   8

Ex. 2 Blues scale
Recipe: 1 X ♭3 4 ♭5 5 X ♭7 8

Observation: If you take away the ♭5 you get a minor pentatonic scale.

6.6. PLAY ALL 12 BLUES SCALES WITH A SWING FEEL

Tip: The swing feel is explained in section 9.3.

C Blues (Go up to high F♯, if you have a high F♯ key)

Blues Scales Practice Log

Play all 12 blues scales from ♪ = 60 to ♪ = 220.

	60	80	100	120	140	160	180	200	220
C									
G									
D									
A									
E									
B									
F#/G♭									
D♭									
A♭									
E♭									
B♭									
F									

6.7. CHAPTER 6 RESEARCH ASSIGNMENTS

The chapter assignments should be a part of your weekly practice routine. Each square (below) equals one hour spent doing research. Copy the template "Analytical Listening" in section 9.16. and use it for each player.

Watching (YouTube)

☐ ☐ ☐ ☐   Ben Webster

☐ ☐ ☐ ☐   Julian "Cannonball" Adderley

☐ ☐ ☐ ☐   Stan Getz

☐ ☐ ☐ ☐   Eric Marienthal

☐ ☐ ☐ ☐   Joshua Redman

Reading (Wikipedia, artist's website, saxophone websites, etc.)

☐ ☐   Ben Webster

☐ ☐   Julian "Cannonball" Adderley

☐ ☐   Stan Getz

☐ ☐   Eric Marienthal

☐ ☐   Joshua Redman

Listening (iTunes, public library, etc.)

☐ ☐ ☐   Ben Webster

☐ ☐ ☐   Julian "Cannonball" Adderley

☐ ☐ ☐   Stan Getz

☐ ☐ ☐   Eric Marienthal

☐ ☐ ☐   Joshua Redman

6.8. TEST: CHAPTER 6

Q1: What is the number formula of the blues scale?

A1:

Q2: What are the notes of the A blues scale?

A2:

Q3: What are the notes of the E blues scale?

A3:

Q4: What are the notes of the F♯ blues scale?

A4:

Q5: What are the notes of the B♭maj9(♯11) chord?

A5:

Q6: What are the notes of the C11 chord?

A6:

Q7: What are the notes of the F9(♯11) chord?

A7:

Q8: What are the notes of the G9(♯5, ♯11) chord?

A8:

Q9: What are the notes of the E♭m11 chord?

A9:

Q10: What are the notes of the Dm11(♭5) chord?

A10:

Do not continue with the next chapter before you have internalized everything from this chapter!

CHAPTER 7

7.1. PLAY ALL MAJOR, HARMONIC, AND MELODIC MINOR SCALES IN DIATONIC SEVENTHS

C Major Scale in Diatonic Sevenths

C Melodic Minor in Diatonic Sevenths

C Harmonic Minor in Diatonic Sevenths

Diatonic Sevenths Practice Log

Play all major (1), harmonic minor (2), and melodic minor (3) scales in diatonic sevenths from ♪ = 60 to ♪ = 220.

	60			80			100			120			140			160			180			200			220		
C	1	2	3																								
G																											
D																											
A																											
E																											
B																											
F#/Gb																											
Db																											
Ab																											
Eb																											
Bb																											
F																											

7.2. PLAY ALL DIATONIC 13TH CHORDS OF THE MAJOR, HARMONIC, AND MELODIC MINOR KEYS

The 13th chords are presented in 7/8 time. This allows for a clean and understandable presentation. Feel free to practice the arpeggios playing eighth notes in 4/4 instead of 7/8 time.

C Major Diatonic Thirteenth Chords – All Ascending

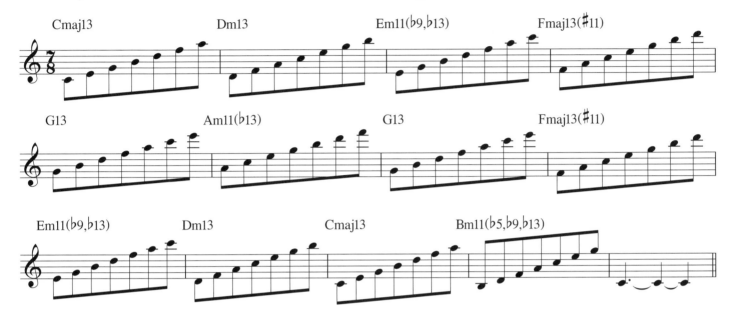

C Major Diatonic Thirteenth Chords – Ascending & Descending

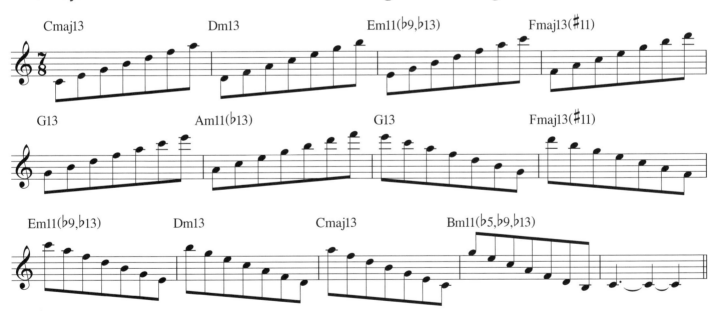

C Melodic Minor Diatonic Thirteenth Chords – All Ascending

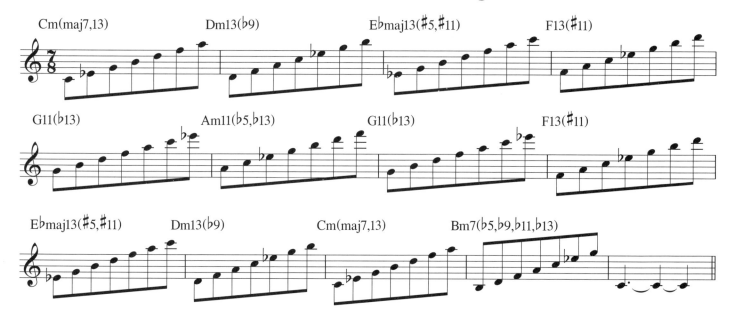

C Melodic Minor Diatonic Thirteenth Chords – Ascending & Descending

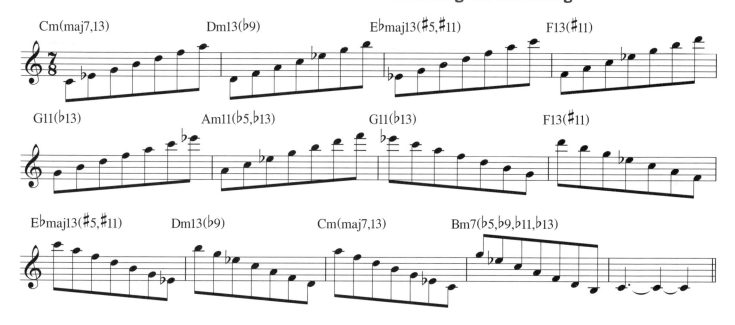

C Harmonic Minor Diatonic Thirteenth Chords – All Ascending

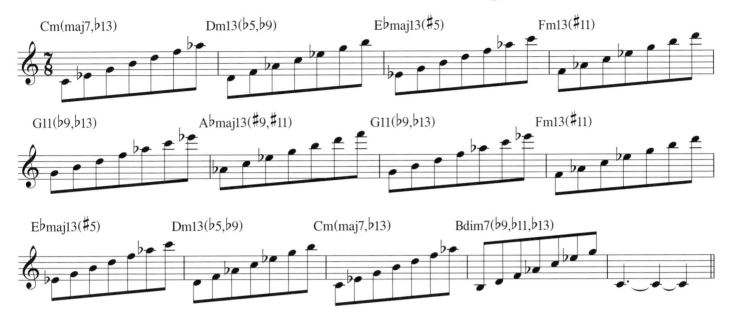

C Harmonic Minor Diatonic Thirteenth Chords – Ascending & Descending

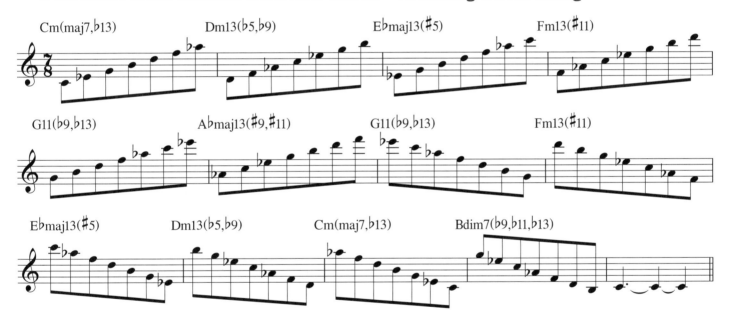

Diatonic Thirteenth Chords Practice Log

Play all diatonic 13th chords of all major (1), harmonic minor (2), and melodic minor (3) keys from ♪ = 60 to ♪ = 220.

	60			80			100			120			140			160			180			200			220		
C	1	2	3																								
G																											
D																											
A																											
E																											
B																											
F#/Gb																											
Db																											
Ab																											
Eb																											
Bb																											
F																											

7.3. PLAY THE 13TH CHORDS ARPEGGIOS

Play all major 13th (#11), dominant 13th (#11), dominant 13th (♭9, #11), minor 13th, minor 7th (♭9, ♭13), minor 7th (♭5, ♭13), and minor 7th (♭5, ♭9, ♭13) chords, using different progressions and cycles.

The progression for the 13th chord examples is moving up in whole steps. Be sure to practice the 13th chords in all progressions/cycles. Remember to use section 9.6. "Regular Progressions Worksheet" in the third part of this book as a guide.

Practice the 13th chord exercises on the entire range of your instrument.

Major Thirteenth (#11) Chords

Dominant Thirteenth (♯11) Chords

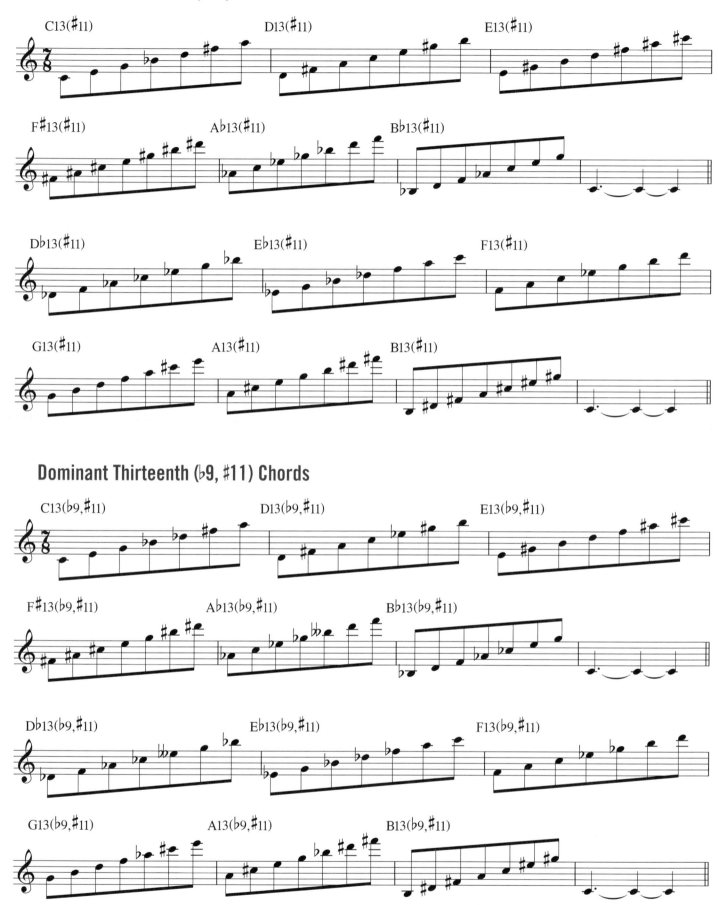

Dominant Thirteenth (♭9, ♯11) Chords

Minor Thirteenth Chords

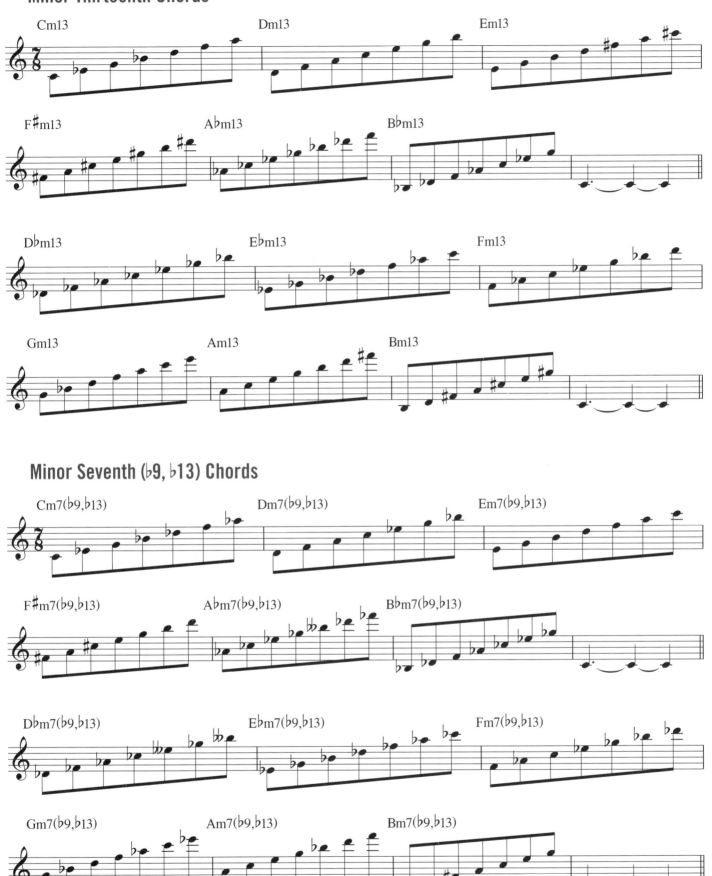

Minor Seventh (♭9, ♭13) Chords

Minor Seventh (♭5, ♭13) Chords

Minor Seventh (♭5, ♭9, ♭13) Chords

Thirteenth Chords Arpeggios Practice Log

Play all major 13th (♯11), dominant 13th (♯11), dominant 13th (♭9, ♯11), minor 13th, minor 7th (♭9, ♭13), minor 7th (♭5, ♭13), and minor 7th (♭5, ♭9, ♭13) chords, using different progressions/cycles from ♪ = 60 to ♪ = 220.

	60	80	100	120	140	160	180	200	220
Maj13(♯11) (1, 3, 5, 7, 9, ♯11, 13)									
Dom13(♯11) (1, 3, 5, ♭7, 9, ♯11, 13)									
Dom13(♭9, ♯11) (1, 3, 5, ♭7, ♭9, ♯11, 13)									
Min13 (1, ♭3, 5, ♭7, 9, 11, 13)								✓	
Min7(♭9, ♭13) (1, ♭3, 5, ♭7, ♭9, 11, ♭13)									
Min7(♭5, ♭13) (1, ♭3, ♭5, ♭7, 9, 11, ♭13)									
Min7(♭5, ♭9, ♭13) (1, ♭3, ♭5, ♭7, ♭9, 11, ♭13)									

7.4. THEORY: WHOLE-TONE SCALES

A whole-tone scale is made up of six different notes. Each note is a whole step from its preceding and succeeding note. The structure of a whole-tone scale is:

$$W - W - W - W - W - W$$

There is a lack of a clear beginning and end in the whole-tone scale due to this very regular and even structure.

There are only two whole-tone scales. Each whole-tone scale can be started on any of the six different notes. This means that by practicing one whole-tone scale, you are actually learning six different scales. What a bargain!

C, D, E, F♯/G♭, G♯/A♭, A♯/B♭ whole-tone scale:

C♯/D♭, D♯/E♭, F, G, A, B whole-tone scale:

7.5. PLAY BOTH WHOLE-TONE SCALES

Play the C, D, E, F♯/G♭, G♯/A♭, A♯/B♭ whole-tone scale from ♪ = 60 to ♪ = 220.

60	80	100	120	140	160	180	200	220

Play the C♯/D♭, D♯/E♭, F, G, A, B whole-tone scale from ♪ = 60 to ♪ = 220.

60	80	100	120	140	160	180	200	220

7.6. THEORY: SYMMETRIC DIMINISHED SCALES

These scales are called symmetric diminished because their structure is the same forwards and backwards. There are two different symmetric diminished structures:

Whole step/half step structure = W-H-W-H-W-H- etc.

Half step/whole step structure = H-W-H-W-H-W- etc.

1. Whole step/half step scales
The C, E♭, F♯, and A whole step/half step scales share the same notes.

The D♭, E, G, and B♭ whole step/half step scales share the same notes.

98

The D, F, A♭, and B whole step/half step scales share the same notes.

2. Half step/whole step scales
The C, E♭, F♯, and A half step/whole step scales share the same notes.

The D♭, E, G, and B♭ half step/whole step scales share the same notes.

The D, F, A♭, and B half step/whole step scales share the same notes.

7.7. PLAY ALL SYMMETRIC DIMINISHED SCALES

Symmetric Diminished Scales Practice Logs

Play the C, Eb, F#, and A whole step/half step form from ♪ = 60 to ♪ = 220.

60	80	100	120	140	160	180	200	220

Play the Db, E, G, and Bb whole step/half step form from ♪ = 60 to ♪ = 220.

60	80	100	120	140	160	180	200	220

Play the D, F, Ab, and B whole step/half step form from ♪ = 60 to ♪ = 220.

60	80	100	120	140	160	180	200	220

Play the C, Eb, F#, and A half step/whole step form from ♪ = 60 to ♪ = 220.

60	80	100	120	140	160	180	200	220

Play the Db, E, G, and Bb half step/whole step form from ♪ = 60 to ♪ = 220.

60	80	100	120	140	160	180	200	220

Play the D, F, Ab, and B half step/whole step form from ♪ = 60 to ♪ = 220.

60	80	100	120	140	160	180	200	220

7.8. THEORY: SHARP ONE AND SHARP TWO DIMINISHED SCALE

The sharp one and sharp two diminished scales are derived from the sharp one and sharp two diminished 7th chord. Both chords function as passing chords.

Ex. 1 Sharp one and sharp two diminished seventh chords (passing chords)

The sharp one and sharp two diminished scale are both made up of eight different notes. Both scales are identical, as they share the same structure (H-W-H-W-W-H-W-H). Therefore, you only must learn 12 scales. Each scale could be a sharp one or a sharp two diminished scale depending of the context (i.e. G#°7 could be the sharp one diminished chord in G Major or the sharp two diminished chord in F Major).

Ex. 2 C# diminished scale

To aid the learning of these scales you may want to think of them as a Mixolydian mode starting on the #1.

7.9. PLAY ALL SHARP ONE AND SHARP TWO DIMINISHED SCALES

Sharp One and Sharp Two Diminished Scales Practice Log

Play all sharp one and sharp two diminished scales from ♪ = 60 to ♪ = 220.

	60		80	100	120	140	160	180	200	220
C	1	2								
G										
D										
A										
E										
B										
F#/G♭										
D♭										
A♭										
E♭										
B♭										
F										

7.10. CHAPTER 7 RESEARCH ASSIGNMENTS

The chapter assignments should be a part of your weekly practice routine. Each square (below) equals one hour spent doing research. Copy the template "Analytical Listening" in section 9.16. and use it for each player.

Watching (YouTube)

☐ ☐ ☐ ☐   Johnny Hodges

☐ ☐ ☐ ☐   Benny Golson

☐ ☐ ☐ ☐   John Coltrane

☐ ☐ ☐ ☐   Charlie Parker

☐ ☐ ☐ ☐   Paquito D'Rivera

Reading (Wikipedia, artist's website, saxophone websites, etc.)

☐ ☐   Johnny Hodges

☐ ☐   Benny Golson

☐ ☐   John Coltrane

☐ ☐   Charlie Parker

☐ ☐   Paquito D'Rivera

Listening (iTunes, public library, etc.)

☐ ☐ ☐   Johnny Hodges

☐ ☐ ☐   Benny Golson

☐ ☐ ☐   John Coltrane

☐ ☐ ☐   Charlie Parker

☐ ☐ ☐   Paquito D'Rivera

7.11. TEST: CHAPTER 7

Q1: What are the notes of the D♭ whole-tone scale?

A1:

Q2: What are the notes of the G whole step/half step symmetric diminished scale?

A2:

Q3: What are the notes of the D♯ diminished scale (sharp one diminished scale)?

A3:

Q4: What are the notes of the A♭maj13(♯11) chord?

A4:

Q5: What are the notes of the F13(♯11) chord?

A5:

Q6: What are the notes of the E13(♭9, ♯11) chord?

A6:

Q7: What are the notes of the F♯m13 chord?

A7:

Q8: What are the notes of the Bm7(♭9, ♭13) chord?

A8:

Q9: What are the notes of the Am7(♭5, ♭13) chord?

A9:

Q10: What are the notes of the Cm7(♭5, ♭9, ♭13) chord?

A10:

Do not continue with the next chapter before you have internalized everything from this chapter!

CHAPTER 8

8.1. THEORY: BEBOP SCALES

Bebop scales are made up of eight different notes. The additional note is an added passing tone (PT). Due to this extra note, all chord tones fall on a downbeat. Having all chord tones on a downbeat emphasizes the harmony. When improvising, avoid playing the passing tones on downbeats.

Ex. 1 Dominant bebop scale

Ex. 2 Dorian bebop scale

Ex. 3 Major bebop scale

Ex. 4 Melodic minor bebop scale

Ex. 5 Harmonic minor bebop scale

8.2. PLAY ALL DOMINANT, DORIAN, MAJOR, MELODIC MINOR, AND HARMONIC MINOR BEBOP SCALES

C Dominant Bebop Scale

Dominant Bebop Scales Practice Log

Play all dominant bebop scales from ♪ = 60 to ♪ = 220.

	60	80	100	120	140	160	180	200	220
C									
G									
D									
A									
E									
B									
F#/Gb									
Db									
Ab									
Eb									
Bb									
F									

C Dorian Bebop Scale

Dorian Bebop Scales Practice Log

Play all Dorian bebop scales from ♪ = 60 to ♪ = 220.

	60	80	100	120	140	160	180	200	220
C									
G									
D									
A									
E									
B									
F#/Gb									
Db									
Ab									
Eb									
Bb									
F									

C Major Bebop Scale

Major Bebop Scales Practice Log

Play all major bebop scales from ♪ = 60 to ♪ = 220.

	60	80	100	120	140	160	180	200	220
C									
G									
D									
A									
E									
B									
F♯/G♭									
D♭									
A♭									
E♭									
B♭									
F									

C Melodic Minor Bebop Scale

Melodic Minor Bebop Scales Practice Log

Play all melodic minor bebop scales from ♪ = 60 to ♪ = 220.

	60	80	100	120	140	160	180	200	220
C									
G									
D									
A									
E									
B									
F#/G♭									
D♭									
A♭									
E♭									
B♭									
F									

C Harmonic Minor Bebop Scale

Harmonic Minor Bebop Scales Practice Log

Play all harmonic minor bebop scales from ♪ = 60 to ♪ = 220.

	60	80	100	120	140	160	180	200	220
C									
G									
D									
A									
E									
B									
F#/G♭									
D♭									
A♭									
E♭									
B♭									
F									

8.3. REVIEWING THIS BOOK USING DIFFERENT RHYTHMS

Make sure you can play all exercises in this book using the following rhythms. If you want to use the practice logs again then just copy the empty practice logs in the section 9.13. "Copy Templates" or simply erase your pencil check marks.

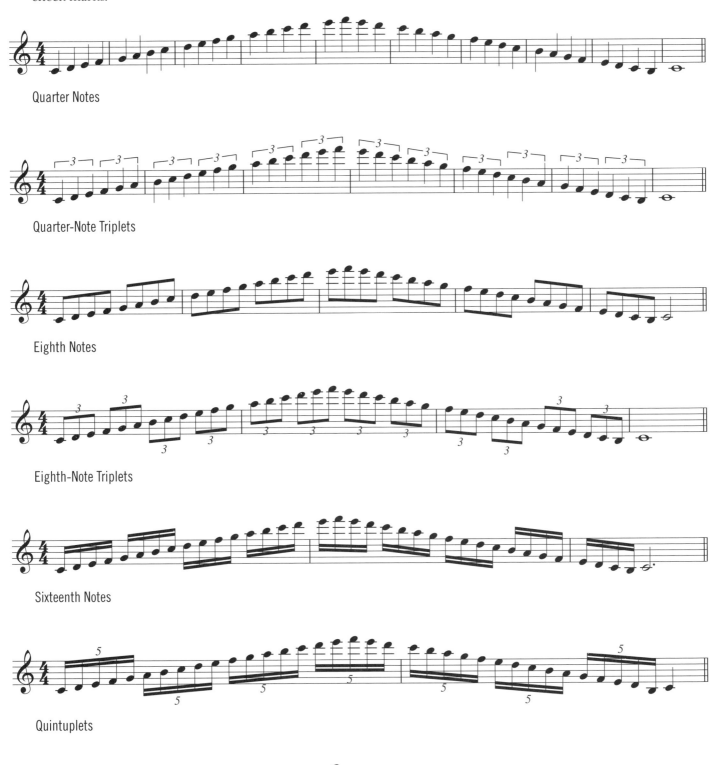

Quarter Notes

Quarter-Note Triplets

Eighth Notes

Eighth-Note Triplets

Sixteenth Notes

Quintuplets

Sextuplets

Septuplets

Thirty-second Notes

8.4. OTHER ASPECTS OF MUSICIANSHIP TO CONSIDER

The purpose of this section is to show you how to continue your technical studies on the saxophone beyond this book. However, as mentioned in the beginning, good technique does not automatically make you a good player. Before you spend a lifetime working solely on saxophone technique, make sure the following aspects of musicianship (listed in alphabetical order) are well-balanced with your technical capabilities:

- analyzing music

- composition and arranging

- ear training and solfège

- gear knowledge and maintenance

- harmony (tonal, modal, and atonal)

- history

- improvisation

- listening to music

- networking (meeting people, getting out of the practice room)

- performances (concerts, auditions, jams, etc.)

- reading and sight-reading

- repertoire (solo and group)

- rhythm

- stylistic interpretation

- theory

- transcriptions

8.5. RECOMMENDED ADVANCED SAXOPHONE TECHNIQUE STUDIES BEYOND THIS BOOK

If, after having consulted the preceding list, you feel you are ready for more advanced saxophone technique, I highly recommend the following books:

Multiphonics, Altissimo Register Playing, Harmonics, Sound Effects

- Caravan, Ronald L., *Preliminary Exercises & Etudes In Contemporary Techniques For Saxophone*, Medfield, Dorn Publications, 1980. Multiphonics, quarter tones, and timbre variation.
- Dörig, Ueli, *Saxophone Sound Effects*, Boston, Berklee Press, 2012. Circular breathing, multiphonics, altissimo register playing, and much more.
- Gross, John, *Multiphonics for the Saxophone*, Rottenburg, Advance Music, 1998. Multiphonics.
- Kientzy, Daniel, *L'art du saxophone*, Paris, Nova-Musica, 1993. Big selection of special effects.
- Luckey, Robert A. Ph.D., *Saxophone Altissimo*, Rottenburg, Advance Music, 1992. Overtones and altissimo register playing.
- Rascher, Sigurd M., *Top-Tones for the Saxophone*, New York, Carl Fischer, 1941. Altissimo register playing.

Scales

- Bergonzi, Jerry, *Hexatonics*, Rottenburg, Advance Music, 2006. Practical method for the construction of Hexatonic (six note) scales.
- Mariano, Charlie, *An Introduction to South Indian Music*, Rottenburg, Advance Music, 2000. Melakartas and TALA-Rhythms.

Advanced Sightreading

- Allard, Joe, *Advanced Rhythms*, New York, Charles Colin Music, 1968. Sightreading, phrasing.
- Dufresne, Gaston, *Develop Sight Reading*, New York, Charles Colin Music. 1972. Sightreading.

Uncommon Patterns, Structures, and Scales in Improvisation

- Campbell, Gary, *Expansions*, Milwaukee, Hal Leonard, 1998.

8.6. CHAPTER 8 RESEARCH ASSIGNMENTS

The chapter assignments should be a part of your weekly practice routine. Each square (below) equals one hour spent doing research. Copy the template "Analytical Listening" in section 9.16. and use it for each player.

Watching (YouTube)

☐ ☐ ☐ ☐   Coleman Hawkins

☐ ☐ ☐ ☐   Lee Konitz

☐ ☐ ☐ ☐   George Garzone

☐ ☐ ☐ ☐   Jan Garbarek

☐ ☐ ☐ ☐   Gerald Albright

Reading (Wikipedia, artist's website, saxophone websites, etc.)

☐ ☐   Coleman Hawkins

☐ ☐   Lee Konitz

☐ ☐   George Garzone

☐ ☐   Jan Garbarek

☐ ☐   Gerald Albright

Listening (iTunes, public library, etc.)

☐ ☐ ☐   Coleman Hawkins

☐ ☐ ☐   Lee Konitz

☐ ☐ ☐   George Garzone

☐ ☐ ☐   Jan Garbarek

☐ ☐ ☐   Gerald Albright

8.7. TEST: CHAPTER 8

Q1: What are the notes of the B dominant bebop scale?

A1:

Q2: What are the notes of the D♭ dominant bebop scale?

A2:

Q3: What are the notes of the G Dorian bebop scale?

A3:

Q4: What are the notes of the E Dorian bebop scale?

A4:

Q5: What are the notes of the A♭ major bebop scale?

A5:

Q6: What are the notes of the F major bebop scale?

A6:

Q7: What are the notes of the B♭ melodic minor bebop scale?

A7:

Q8: What are the notes of the D melodic minor bebop scale?

A8:

Q9: What are the notes of the A harmonic minor bebop scale?

A9:

Q10: This book wasn't too easy, was it?

A10:

PART 3: PRACTICE TOOLBOX

9.1. SCALES OVERVIEW

Scale	Scale Degrees									Characteristic Note(s)
Major	1	2	3	4	5	6	7	8		–
Melodic Minor	1	2	♭3	4	5	6	7	8		♭3
Harmonic Minor	1	2	♭3	4	5	♭6	7	8		♭3, ♭6
Natural Minor	1	2	♭3	4	5	♭6	♭7	8		♭3, ♭6, ♭7
Blues	1		♭3	4	♭5 5		♭7	8		no 2, ♭3, ♭5 & 5, no 6, ♭7
Major Pentatonic	1	2	3		5	6		8		no 4, no 7
Minor Pentatonic	1		♭3	4	5		♭7	8		no 2, ♭3, no 6, ♭7
Symmetric Diminished (Half Step/Whole Step)	1	♭2	♭3	3 #4	5	6	♭7	8		H-W-H-W-H-W-H-W
Symmetric Diminished (Whole Step/Half Step)	1	2	♭3	4	♭5	♭6 6	7	8		W-H-W-H-W-H-W-H
Whole-Tone	1	2	3	#4	#5	#6		8		W-W-W-W-W-W
Ionian (Major)	1	2	3	4	5	6	7	8		
Dorian	1	2	♭3	4	5	6	♭7	8		♭3
Phrygian	1	♭2	♭3	4	5	♭6	♭7	8		♭2
Lydian	1	2	3	#4	5	6	7	8		#4
Mixolydian	1	2	3	4	5	6	♭7	8		♭7
Aeolian (Natural Minor)	1	2	♭3	4	5	♭6	♭7	8		♭6
Locrian	1	♭2	♭3	4	♭5	♭6	♭7	8		♭5
Locrian #6	1	♭2	♭3	4	♭5	6	♭7	8		natural 6
Ionian Augmented	1	2	3	4	#5	6	7	8		#5
Romanian	1	2	♭3	#4	5	6	♭7	8		♭3, #4, ♭7
Phrygian Dominant	1	♭2	3	4	5	♭6	♭7	8		natural 3
Lydian #2	1	#2	3	#4	5	6	7	8		#2
Ultralocrian	1	♭2	♭3	♭4	♭5	♭6	♭♭7	8		♭4, ♭♭7
Dorian ♭9	1	♭2	♭3	4	5	6	♭7	8		♭2
Lydian Augmented	1	2	3	#4	#5	6	7	8		#4, #5
Lydian Dominant	1	2	3	#4	5	6	♭7	8		#4, ♭7
Mixolydian ♭6	1	2	3	4	5	♭6	♭7	8		natural 3, ♭6, ♭7
Semilocrian	1	2	♭3	4	♭5	♭6	♭7	8		natural 2
Superlocrian	1	♭2	♭3	♭4	♭5	♭6	♭7	8		♭4
Melakartas	Check the recommended books in Chapter 8.									

This is not a complete list!

9.2. CIRCLE OF FIFTHS / CIRCLE OF FOURTHS

The circle of fifths follows the circle clockwise. The circle of fourths follows the circle counterclockwise. For each key signature, the major key is shown outside the circle as a capital letter, and the minor key is shown inside the circle as a lower case letter. If you move three places counterclockwise from a major key, you get the key signature of the relative minor key (i.e. C natural minor gets three flats: B♭, E♭, and A♭).

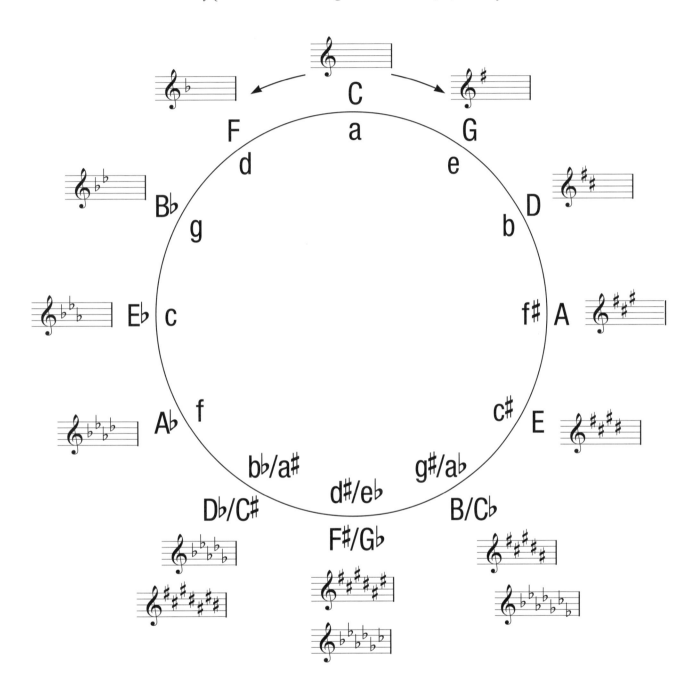

9.3. SWING FEEL

There is no visual difference in music notation between straight eighth notes and swinging eighth notes. If the eighth notes in the music need to be swung then this will be indicated either on the top of the first measure with the word "Swing" or it will be indicated by the context of the music style, such as a jazz standard.

The best way to learn the different swing feels (i.e. swinging hard, swinging soft) is to listen to great jazz music. Actually, it is the only way to really learn how to swing. For some students it might be helpful to visualize the concept of swinging eighth notes. You can also use the following examples as a guide for how to discover the swing feel when listening to jazz music.

1st Step: Note duration

All straight eighth notes get the same duration unless otherwise indicated by articulation marks (i.e. staccato, tenuto, marcato).

Swinging eighth notes are different. Although all swinging eighth notes are written the same, the eighth notes on the downbeat are being played longer than the eighth notes on the upbeat. The bigger the difference of the duration between downbeat and upbeat eighth notes is the harder you swing. Again, listen to different jazz music to hear how the degree of long eighth notes vs. short eighth notes varies.

2nd Step: Accented notes

The problem with the step one is that if you play eighth notes that way, it sounds very "jumpy". That's because the wrong notes get accented. Let's correct that:

Straight eighth notes (classical music)

The accents are on the downbeats (1, 2, 3, 4)

Swinging eighth notes

The accents are on the upbeats (1 & 2 & 3 & 4 &)

The accented upbeats propel the music forward and give it energy. This is one of the reasons why jazz music was so popular for dancing. Often, phrases or licks start on an upbeat (like a pickup eighth note).

3rd Step: Sing swinging eighth notes

It is tremendously helpful to be able to sing (or scat) swinging eighth notes.

Doo = unaccented, long eighth note on a downbeat

Ba = accented, short eighth note on a upbeat

Ba ‖ Doo Ba Doo Ba Doo Ba Doo Ba | Doo Ba Doo Ba Doo Ba Doo Ba ‖

& ‖ 1 & 2 & 3 & 4 & | 1 & 2 & 3 & 4 & ‖

    The next logical (and fun) step is to sing along to great jazz music, and/or to try the concept of swinging eighth notes with your horn.

9.4. TIPS FOR AUDITIONS

1. Walk on stage with confidence. Walk like you belong there. It helps to look at the audience or jury and to give a smile or a nod.

2. It is preferable more and professional to memorize the music and avoid using a music stand. However, if you are using a music stand, make sure it is low enough so the audience or jury can see your face.

3. Take a deep breath to relax your body.

4. Ensure you have the first two to four measures ready to go. Sing them in your head to be sure about the tempo.

5. If you'd like, you may announce your song to the audience.

6. While performing, bend your knees slightly. This will help you stay loose and encourage blood flow, preventing fainting.

7. If you make a mistake, keep going. Don't stop, and don't make a face.

8. If you perform more than one piece, pause between them, and thank the audience or jury with a smile.

9. When your performance is over, don't rush off the stage. Smile and take a bow. If you played with an accompanist, acknowledge him or her. After your accompanist takes a bow, walk off the stage with a smile, knowing that you have done a great job.

10. Always have a backup reed ready. Not being able to perform because your reed just cracked sounds like "My dog ate my homework." Always be prepared for the worst case.

If there is a microphone involved:

11. Wait until the microphone has been adjusted before you begin.

12. Remember to stay close to the microphone. Be sure you can hear yourself in the speaker monitor.

9.5. SAXOPHONE PLAYERS TO CHECK OUT

Because many saxophone players double on clarinet and/or flute, it seems more logical to make this a wood-wind player list, rather than exclusively a saxophone player list. Please note that the musicians were given an "x" for the instrument(s) that they are known for, which doesn't necessarily mean they don't or didn't play other instruments.

F = Flute		T = Tenor		S = Soprano			
C = Clarinet		A = Alto		B = Baritone			

	F	C	T	A	S	B	Chapter
Ben Webster			X				6
Benny Carter				X			3
Benny Golson			X				7
Bob Mintzer			X		X		1
Branford Marsalis			X		X		5
Cannonball Adderley				X			6
Charlie Mariano				X			-
Charlie Parker				X			7
Chris Potter			X		X		-
Coleman Hawkins			X				8
Dave Liebman	X		X		X		5
David Sanborn				X			2
Dexter Gordon			X		X		4
Earl Bostic				X			3
Eric Dolphy	X	X		X			4
Eric Marienthal			X	X	X		6
Gerry Mulligan						X	5
George Garzone			X		X		8
Gerald Albright				X	X		8
Greg Osby				X	X		2
Grover Washington Jr.				X	X		1
Jan Garbarek			X		X		8
Jerry Bergonzi			X		X		4
Joe Henderson			X				-
Joe Lovano			X		X		3
John Coltrane			X		X		7
Johnny Hodges				X			7
Joshua Redman			X		X		6
Kenny Garrett				X	X		1
Lee Konitz				X			8
Lennie Niehaus				X			-
Lester Young			X		X		2
Maceo Parker				X			4
Michael Brecker			X				3
Oliver Nelson			X				2

	F	C	T	A	S	B	Chapter
Ornette Coleman				X			-
Paquito D'Rivera		X		X			7
Paul Desmond				X			4
Phil Woods				X			3
Roland Kirk	X		X	X	X		1
Serge Chaloff						X	-
Sidney Bechet		X			X		1
Sonny Rollins			X		X		5
Sonny Stitt			X				5
Stan Getz			X				6
Steve Grossman			X				-
Tom Scott			X		X		-
Walter Beasley				X	X		-
Wayne Shorter			X		X		2
Yusef Latif	X		X				-

Thanks to Jeff Harrington for his help in compiling this list. For more on Jeff's great saxophone education visit: www.jeffharrington.com

This is not a complete list!

9.6. REGULAR PROGRESSIONS WORKSHEET

½ step up	C	C#	D	Eb	E	F	F#	G	G#	A	Bb	B
½ step down	C	B	Bb	A	Ab	G	F#	F	E	Eb	D	C#
Step up	C	D	E	F#	G#	Bb	C#	Eb	F	G	A	B
Step down	C	Bb	Ab	F#	E	D	C#	B	A	G	F	Eb
Min 3rd up	C	Eb	F#	A	C#	E	G	Bb	D	F	Ab	B
Min 3rd down	C	A	F#	Eb	C#	Bb	G	E	D	B	Ab	F
Maj 3rd up	C	E	G#	C#	F	A	D	F#	Bb	Eb	G	B
Maj 3rd down	C	G#	E	C#	A	F	D	Bb	F#	Eb	B	G
4th up	C	F	Bb	Eb	Ab	C#	F#	B	E	A	D	G
4th down	C	G	D	A	E	B	F#	C#	Ab	Eb	Bb	F
5th up	C	G	D	A	E	B	F#	C#	Ab	Eb	Bb	F
5th down	C	F	Bb	Eb	Ab	C#	F#	B	E	A	D	G
Min 6th up	C	Ab	E	C#	A	F	D	Bb	F#	Eb	B	G
Min 6th down	C	E	G#	C#	F	A	D	F#	Bb	Eb	G	B
Maj 6th up	C	A	F#	Eb	C#	Bb	G	E	D	B	Ab	F
Maj 6th down	C	Eb	F#	A	C#	E	G	Bb	D	F	Ab	B
Min 7th up	C	Bb	Ab	F#	E	D	C#	B	A	G	F	Eb
Min 7th down	C	D	E	F#	G#	Bb	C#	Eb	F	G	A	B
Maj 7th up	C	B	Bb	A	Ab	G	F#	F	E	Eb	D	C#
Maj 7th down	C	C#	D	Eb	E	F	F#	G	G#	A	Bb	B

9.7. RANDOM PROGRESSIONS WORKSHEET

Work in all directions: Right to left, left to right, diagonally, as well as up and down.

C	F	F#	A♭	B	D	C#	G	E♭	B♭	A	E
A♭	F#	E♭	G	E	C#	C	B♭	D	F	B	A
G	B♭	C#	E♭	A	D	F	C	A♭	E	F#	B
B	C#	F	B♭	A	C	E♭	D	A♭	F#	G	E
E	G	B♭	C#	F#	E♭	B	A	C	A♭	D	F
E♭	C	F	E	G	B♭	A	C#	B	A♭	D	F#
F#	B	G	C	A♭	A	C#	E	F	D	B♭	E♭
A	F#	B♭	D	B	F	C	E	C#	A♭	G	E♭
D	G	B♭	A	B	E♭	C#	A♭	E	F#	C	F
F	C#	A♭	B♭	C	G	B	E♭	F#	A	E	D
C#	E♭	A♭	B♭	B	E	G	A	F	C	D	F#
B♭	C#	G	A♭	F	E♭	E	C	A	F#	B	D

125

9.8. MAJOR 7TH CHORDS REGULAR PROGRESSIONS WORKSHEET

½ step up	C^{maj7}	C#^{maj7}	D^{maj7}	E♭^{maj7}	E^{maj7}	F^{maj7}	F#^{maj7}	G^{maj7}	G#^{maj7}	A^{maj7}	B♭^{maj7}	B^{maj7}
½ step down	C^{maj7}	B^{maj7}	B♭^{maj7}	A^{maj7}	A♭^{maj7}	G^{maj7}	F#^{maj7}	F^{maj7}	E^{maj7}	E♭^{maj7}	D^{maj7}	C#^{maj7}
Step up	C^{maj7}	D^{maj7}	E^{maj7}	F#^{maj7}	G#^{maj7}	B♭^{maj7}	C#^{maj7}	E♭^{maj7}	F^{maj7}	G^{maj7}	A^{maj7}	B^{maj7}
Step down	C^{maj7}	B♭^{maj7}	A♭^{maj7}	F#^{maj7}	E^{maj7}	D^{maj7}	C#^{maj7}	B^{maj7}	A^{maj7}	G^{maj7}	F^{maj7}	E♭^{maj7}
Min 3rd up	C^{maj7}	E♭^{maj7}	F#^{maj7}	A^{maj7}	C#^{maj7}	E^{maj7}	G^{maj7}	B♭^{maj7}	D^{maj7}	F^{maj7}	A♭^{maj7}	B^{maj7}
Min 3rd down	C^{maj7}	A^{maj7}	F#^{maj7}	E♭^{maj7}	C#^{maj7}	B♭^{maj7}	G^{maj7}	E^{maj7}	D^{maj7}	B^{maj7}	A♭^{maj7}	F^{maj7}
Maj 3rd up	C^{maj7}	E^{maj7}	G#^{maj7}	C#^{maj7}	F^{maj7}	A^{maj7}	D^{maj7}	F#^{maj7}	B♭^{maj7}	E♭^{maj7}	G^{maj7}	B^{maj7}
Maj 3rd down	C^{maj7}	G#^{maj7}	E^{maj7}	C#^{maj7}	A^{maj7}	F^{maj7}	D^{maj7}	B♭^{maj7}	F#^{maj7}	E♭^{maj7}	B^{maj7}	G^{maj7}
4th up	C^{maj7}	F^{maj7}	B♭^{maj7}	E♭^{maj7}	A♭^{maj7}	C#^{maj7}	F#^{maj7}	B^{maj7}	E^{maj7}	A^{maj7}	D^{maj7}	G^{maj7}
4th down	C^{maj7}	G^{maj7}	D^{maj7}	A^{maj7}	E^{maj7}	B^{maj7}	F#^{maj7}	C#^{maj7}	A♭^{maj7}	E♭^{maj7}	B♭^{maj7}	F^{maj7}
5th up	C^{maj7}	G^{maj7}	D^{maj7}	A^{maj7}	E^{maj7}	B^{maj7}	F#^{maj7}	C#^{maj7}	A♭^{maj7}	E♭^{maj7}	B♭^{maj7}	F^{maj7}
5th down	C^{maj7}	F^{maj7}	B♭^{maj7}	E♭^{maj7}	A♭^{maj7}	C#^{maj7}	F#^{maj7}	B^{maj7}	E^{maj7}	A^{maj7}	D^{maj7}	G^{maj7}
Min 6th up	C^{maj7}	A♭^{maj7}	E^{maj7}	C#^{maj7}	A^{maj7}	F^{maj/}	D^{maj7}	B♭^{maj7}	F#^{maj7}	E♭^{maj7}	B^{maj7}	G^{maj7}
Min 6th down	C^{maj7}	E^{maj7}	G#^{maj7}	C#^{maj7}	F^{maj7}	A^{maj7}	D^{maj7}	F#^{maj7}	B♭^{maj7}	E♭^{maj7}	G^{maj7}	B^{maj7}
Maj 6th up	C^{maj7}	A^{maj7}	F#^{maj7}	E♭^{maj7}	C#^{maj7}	B♭^{maj7}	G^{maj7}	E^{maj7}	D^{maj7}	B^{maj7}	A♭^{maj7}	F^{maj7}
Maj 6th down	C^{maj7}	E♭^{maj7}	F#^{maj7}	A^{maj7}	C#^{maj7}	E^{maj7}	G^{maj7}	B♭^{maj7}	D^{maj7}	F^{maj7}	A♭^{maj7}	B^{maj7}
Min 7th up	C^{maj7}	B♭^{maj7}	A♭^{maj7}	F#^{maj7}	E^{maj7}	D^{maj7}	C#^{maj7}	B^{maj7}	A^{maj7}	G^{maj7}	F^{maj7}	E♭^{maj7}
Min 7th down	C^{maj7}	D^{maj7}	E^{maj7}	F#^{maj7}	G#^{maj7}	B♭^{maj7}	C#^{maj7}	E♭^{maj7}	F^{maj7}	G^{maj7}	A^{maj7}	B^{maj7}
Maj 7th up	C^{maj7}	B^{maj7}	B♭^{maj7}	A^{maj7}	A♭^{maj7}	G^{maj7}	F#^{maj7}	F^{maj7}	E^{maj7}	E♭^{maj7}	D^{maj7}	C#^{maj7}
Maj 7th down	C^{maj7}	C#^{maj7}	D^{maj7}	E♭^{maj7}	E^{maj7}	F^{maj7}	F#^{maj7}	G^{maj7}	G#^{maj7}	A^{maj7}	B♭^{maj7}	B^{maj7}

9.9. DOMINANT 7TH CHORDS REGULAR PROGRESSIONS WORKSHEET

½ step up	C⁷	C#⁷	D⁷	E♭⁷	E⁷	F⁷	F#⁷	G⁷	G#⁷	A⁷	B♭⁷	B⁷
½ step down	C⁷	B⁷	B♭⁷	A⁷	A♭⁷	G⁷	F#⁷	F⁷	E⁷	E♭⁷	D⁷	C#⁷
Step up	C⁷	D⁷	E⁷	F#⁷	G#⁷	B♭⁷	C#⁷	E♭⁷	F⁷	G⁷	A⁷	B⁷
Step down	C⁷	B♭⁷	A♭⁷	F#⁷	E⁷	D⁷	C#⁷	B⁷	A⁷	G⁷	F⁷	E♭⁷
Min 3rd up	C⁷	E♭⁷	F#⁷	A⁷	C#⁷	E⁷	G⁷	B♭⁷	D⁷	F⁷	A♭⁷	B⁷
Min 3rd down	C⁷	A⁷	F#⁷	E♭⁷	C#⁷	B♭⁷	G⁷	E⁷	D⁷	B⁷	A♭⁷	F⁷
Maj 3rd up	C⁷	E⁷	G#⁷	C#⁷	F⁷	A⁷	D⁷	F#⁷	B♭⁷	E♭⁷	G⁷	B⁷
Maj 3rd down	C⁷	G#⁷	E⁷	C#⁷	A⁷	F⁷	D⁷	B♭⁷	F#⁷	E♭⁷	B⁷	G⁷
4th up	C⁷	F⁷	B♭⁷	E♭⁷	A♭⁷	C#⁷	F#⁷	B⁷	E⁷	A⁷	D⁷	G⁷
4th down	C⁷	G⁷	D⁷	A⁷	E⁷	B⁷	F#⁷	C#⁷	A♭⁷	E♭⁷	B♭⁷	F⁷
5th up	C⁷	G⁷	D⁷	A⁷	E⁷	B⁷	F#⁷	C#⁷	A♭⁷	E♭⁷	B♭⁷	F⁷
5th down	C⁷	F⁷	B♭⁷	E♭⁷	A♭⁷	C#⁷	F#⁷	B⁷	E⁷	A⁷	D⁷	G⁷
Min 6th up	C⁷	A♭⁷	E⁷	C#⁷	A⁷	F⁷	D⁷	B♭⁷	F#⁷	E♭⁷	B⁷	G⁷
Min 6th down	C⁷	E⁷	G#⁷	C#⁷	F⁷	A⁷	D⁷	F#⁷	B♭⁷	E♭⁷	G⁷	B⁷
Maj 6th up	C⁷	A⁷	F#⁷	E♭⁷	C#⁷	B♭⁷	G⁷	E⁷	D⁷	B⁷	A♭⁷	F⁷
Maj 6th down	C⁷	E♭⁷	F#⁷	A⁷	C#⁷	E⁷	G⁷	B♭⁷	D⁷	F⁷	A♭⁷	B⁷
Min 7th up	C⁷	B♭⁷	A♭⁷	F#⁷	E⁷	D⁷	C#⁷	B⁷	A⁷	G⁷	F⁷	E♭⁷
Min 7th down	C⁷	D⁷	E⁷	F#⁷	G#⁷	B♭⁷	C#⁷	E♭⁷	F⁷	G⁷	A⁷	B⁷
Maj 7th up	C⁷	B⁷	B♭⁷	A⁷	A♭⁷	G⁷	F#⁷	F⁷	E⁷	E♭⁷	D⁷	C#⁷
Maj 7th down	C⁷	C#⁷	D⁷	E♭⁷	E⁷	F⁷	F#⁷	G⁷	G#⁷	A⁷	B♭⁷	B⁷

9.10. MINOR 7TH CHORDS REGULAR PROGRESSIONS WORKSHEET

½ step up	C^{m7}	C#^{m7}	D^{m7}	E♭^{m7}	E^{m7}	F^{m7}	F#^{m7}	G^{m7}	G#^{m7}	A^{m7}	B♭^{m7}	B^{m7}
½ step down	C^{m7}	B^{m7}	B♭^{m7}	A^{m7}	A♭^{m7}	G^{m7}	F#^{m7}	F^{m7}	E^{m7}	E♭^{m7}	D^{m7}	C#^{m7}
Step up	C^{m7}	D^{m7}	E^{m7}	F#^{m7}	G#^{m7}	B♭^{m7}	C#^{m7}	E♭^{m7}	F^{m7}	G^{m7}	A^{m7}	B^{m7}
Step down	C^{m7}	B♭^{m7}	A♭^{m7}	F#^{m7}	E^{m7}	D^{m7}	C#^{m7}	B^{m7}	A^{m7}	G^{m7}	F^{m7}	E♭^{m7}
Min 3rd up	C^{m7}	E♭^{m7}	F#^{m7}	A^{m7}	C#^{m7}	E^{m7}	G^{m7}	B♭^{m7}	D^{m7}	F^{m7}	A♭^{m7}	B^{m7}
Min 3rd down	C^{m7}	A^{m7}	F#^{m7}	E♭^{m7}	C#^{m7}	B♭^{m7}	G^{m7}	E^{m7}	D^{m7}	B^{m7}	A♭^{m7}	F^{m7}
Maj 3rd up	C^{m7}	E^{m7}	G#^{m7}	C#^{m7}	F^{m7}	A^{m7}	D^{m7}	F#^{m7}	B♭^{m7}	E♭^{m7}	G^{m7}	B^{m7}
Maj 3rd down	C^{m7}	G#^{m7}	E^{m7}	C#^{m7}	A^{m7}	F^{m7}	D^{m7}	B♭^{m7}	F#^{m7}	E♭^{m7}	B^{m7}	G^{m7}
4th up	C^{m7}	F^{m7}	B♭^{m7}	E♭^{m7}	A♭^{m7}	C#^{m7}	F#^{m7}	B^{m7}	E^{m7}	A^{m7}	D^{m7}	G^{m7}
4th down	C^{m7}	G^{m7}	D^{m7}	A^{m7}	E^{m7}	B^{m7}	F#^{m7}	C#^{m7}	A♭^{m7}	E♭^{m7}	B♭^{m7}	F^{m7}
5th up	C^{m7}	G^{m7}	D^{m7}	A^{m7}	E^{m7}	B^{m7}	F#^{m7}	C#^{m7}	A♭^{m7}	E♭^{m7}	B♭^{m7}	F^{m7}
5th down	C^{m7}	F^{m7}	B♭^{m7}	E♭^{m7}	A♭^{m7}	C#^{m7}	F#^{m7}	B^{m7}	E^{m7}	A^{m7}	D^{m7}	G^{m7}
Min 6th up	C^{m7}	A♭^{m7}	E^{m7}	C#^{m7}	A^{m7}	F^{m7}	D^{m7}	B♭^{m7}	F#^{m7}	E♭^{m7}	B^{m7}	G^{m7}
Min 6th down	C^{m7}	E^{m7}	G#^{m7}	C#^{m7}	F^{m7}	A^{m7}	D^{m7}	F#^{m7}	B♭^{m7}	E♭^{m7}	G^{m7}	B^{m7}
Maj 6th up	C^{m7}	A^{m7}	F#^{m7}	E♭^{m7}	C#^{m7}	B♭^{m7}	G^{m7}	E^{m7}	D^{m7}	B^{m7}	A♭^{m7}	F^{m7}
Maj 6th down	C^{m7}	E♭^{m7}	F#^{m7}	A^{m7}	C#^{m7}	E^{m7}	G^{m7}	B♭^{m7}	D^{m7}	F^{m7}	A♭^{m7}	B^{m7}
Min 7th up	C^{m7}	B♭^{m7}	A♭^{m7}	F#^{m7}	E^{m7}	D^{m7}	C#^{m7}	B^{m7}	A^{m7}	G^{m7}	F^{m7}	E♭^{m7}
Min 7th down	C^{m7}	D^{m7}	E^{m7}	F#^{m7}	G#^{m7}	B♭^{m7}	C#^{m7}	E♭^{m7}	F^{m7}	G^{m7}	A^{m7}	B^{m7}
Maj 7th up	C^{m7}	B^{m7}	B♭^{m7}	A^{m7}	A♭^{m7}	G^{m7}	F#^{m7}	F^{m7}	E^{m7}	E♭^{m7}	D^{m7}	C#^{m7}
Maj 7th down	C^{m7}	C#^{m7}	D^{m7}	E♭^{m7}	E^{m7}	F^{m7}	F#^{m7}	G^{m7}	G#^{m7}	A^{m7}	B♭^{m7}	B^{m7}

9.11. MINOR 7TH (♭5) CHORDS REGULAR PROGRESSIONS WORKSHEET

½ step up	$C^{m7(\flat5)}$	$C\#^{m7(\flat5)}$	$D^{m7(\flat5)}$	$E\flat^{m7(\flat5)}$	$E^{m7(\flat5)}$	$F^{m7(\flat5)}$	$F\#^{m7(\flat5)}$	$G^{m7(\flat5)}$	$G\#^{m7(\flat5)}$	$A^{m7(\flat5)}$	$B\flat^{m7(\flat5)}$	$B^{m7(\flat5)}$
½ step down	$C^{m7(\flat5)}$	$B^{m7(\flat5)}$	$B\flat^{m7(\flat5)}$	$A^{m7(\flat5)}$	$A\flat^{m7(\flat5)}$	$G^{m7(\flat5)}$	$F\#^{m7(\flat5)}$	$F^{m7(\flat5)}$	$E^{m7(\flat5)}$	$E\flat^{m7(\flat5)}$	$D^{m7(\flat5)}$	$C\#^{m7(\flat5)}$
Step up	$C^{m7(\flat5)}$	$D^{m7(\flat5)}$	$E^{m7(\flat5)}$	$F\#^{m7(\flat5)}$	$G\#^{m7(\flat5)}$	$B\flat^{m7(\flat5)}$	$C\#^{m7(\flat5)}$	$E\flat^{m7(\flat5)}$	$F^{m7(\flat5)}$	$G^{m7(\flat5)}$	$A^{m7(\flat5)}$	$B^{m7(\flat5)}$
Step down	$C^{m7(\flat5)}$	$B\flat^{m7(\flat5)}$	$A\flat^{m7(\flat5)}$	$F\#^{m7(\flat5)}$	$E^{m7(\flat5)}$	$D^{m7(\flat5)}$	$C\#^{m7(\flat5)}$	$B^{m7(\flat5)}$	$A^{m7(\flat5)}$	$G^{m7(\flat5)}$	$F^{m7(\flat5)}$	$E\flat^{m7(\flat5)}$
Min 3rd up	$C^{m7(\flat5)}$	$E\flat^{m7(\flat5)}$	$F\#^{m7(\flat5)}$	$A^{m7(\flat5)}$	$C\#^{m7(\flat5)}$	$E^{m7(\flat5)}$	$G^{m7(\flat5)}$	$B\flat^{m7(\flat5)}$	$D^{m7(\flat5)}$	$F^{m7(\flat5)}$	$A\flat^{m7(\flat5)}$	$B^{m7(\flat5)}$
Min 3rd down	$C^{m7(\flat5)}$	$A^{m7(\flat5)}$	$F\#^{m7(\flat5)}$	$E\flat^{m7(\flat5)}$	$C\#^{m7}$	$B\flat^{m7(\flat5)}$	$G^{m7(\flat5)}$	E^{m7}	$D^{m7(\flat5)}$	$B^{m7(\flat5)}$	$A\flat^{m7(\flat5)}$	$F^{m7(\flat5)}$
Maj 3rd up	$C^{m7(\flat5)}$	$E^{m7(\flat5)}$	$G\#^{m7(\flat5)}$	$C\#^{m7(\flat5)}$	$F^{m7(\flat5)}$	$A^{m7(\flat5)}$	$D^{m7(\flat5)}$	$F\#^{m7(\flat5)}$	$B\flat^{m7(\flat5)}$	$E\flat^{m7(\flat5)}$	$G^{m7(\flat5)}$	$B^{m7(\flat5)}$
Maj 3rd down	$C^{m7(\flat5)}$	$G\#^{m7(\flat5)}$	$E^{m7(\flat5)}$	$C\#^{m7(\flat5)}$	$A^{m7(\flat5)}$	$F^{m7(\flat5)}$	$D^{m7(\flat5)}$	$B\flat^{m7(\flat5)}$	$F\#^{m7(\flat5)}$	$E\flat^{m7(\flat5)}$	$B^{m7(\flat5)}$	$G^{m7(\flat5)}$
4th up	$C^{m7(\flat5)}$	$F^{m7(\flat5)}$	$B\flat^{m7(\flat5)}$	$E\flat^{m7(\flat5)}$	$A\flat^{m7(\flat5)}$	$C\#^{m7(\flat5)}$	$F\#^{m7(\flat5)}$	$B^{m7(\flat5)}$	$E^{m7(\flat5)}$	$A^{m7(\flat5)}$	$D^{m7(\flat5)}$	$G^{m7(\flat5)}$
4th down	$C^{m7(\flat5)}$	$G^{m7(\flat5)}$	$D^{m7(\flat5)}$	$A^{m7(\flat5)}$	$E^{m7(\flat5)}$	$B^{m7(\flat5)}$	$F\#^{m7(\flat5)}$	$C\#^{m7(\flat5)}$	$A\flat^{m7(\flat5)}$	$E\flat^{m7(\flat5)}$	$B\flat^{m7(\flat5)}$	$F^{m7(\flat5)}$
5th up	$C^{m7(\flat5)}$	$G^{m7(\flat5)}$	$D^{m7(\flat5)}$	$A^{m7(\flat5)}$	$E^{m7(\flat5)}$	$B^{m7(\flat5)}$	$F\#^{m7(\flat5)}$	$C\#^{m7(\flat5)}$	$A\flat^{m7(\flat5)}$	$E\flat^{m7(\flat5)}$	$B\flat^{m7(\flat5)}$	$F^{m7(\flat5)}$
5th down	$C^{m7(\flat5)}$	$F^{m7(\flat5)}$	$B\flat^{m7(\flat5)}$	$E\flat^{m7(\flat5)}$	$A\flat^{m7(\flat5)}$	$C\#^{m7(\flat5)}$	$F\#^{m7(\flat5)}$	$B^{m7(\flat5)}$	$E^{m7(\flat5)}$	$A^{m7(\flat5)}$	$D^{m7(\flat5)}$	$G^{m7(\flat5)}$
Min 6th up	$C^{m7(\flat5)}$	$A\flat^{m7(\flat5)}$	$E^{m7(\flat5)}$	$C\#^{m7(\flat5)}$	$A^{m7(\flat5)}$	$F^{m7(\flat5)}$	$D^{m7(\flat5)}$	$B\flat^{m7(\flat5)}$	$F\#^{m7(\flat5)}$	$E\flat^{m7(\flat5)}$	$B^{m7(\flat5)}$	$G^{m7(\flat5)}$
Min 6th down	$C^{m7(\flat5)}$	$E^{m7(\flat5)}$	$G\#^{m7(\flat5)}$	$C\#^{m7(\flat5)}$	$F^{m7(\flat5)}$	$A^{m7(\flat5)}$	$D^{m7(\flat5)}$	$F\#^{m7(\flat5)}$	$B\flat^{m7(\flat5)}$	$E\flat^{m7(\flat5)}$	$G^{m7(\flat5)}$	$B^{m7(\flat5)}$
Maj 6th up	$C^{m7(\flat5)}$	$A^{m7(\flat5)}$	$F\#^{m7(\flat5)}$	$E\flat^{m7(\flat5)}$	$C\#^{m7(\flat5)}$	$B\flat^{m7(\flat5)}$	$G^{m7(\flat5)}$	$E^{m7(\flat5)}$	$D^{m7(\flat5)}$	$B^{m7(\flat5)}$	$A\flat^{m7(\flat5)}$	$F^{m7(\flat5)}$
Maj 6th down	$C^{m7(\flat5)}$	$E\flat^{m7(\flat5)}$	$F\#^{m7(\flat5)}$	$A^{m7(\flat5)}$	$C\#^{m7(\flat5)}$	$E^{m7(\flat5)}$	$G^{m7(\flat5)}$	$B\flat^{m7(\flat5)}$	$D^{m7(\flat5)}$	$F^{m7(\flat5)}$	$A\flat^{m7(\flat5)}$	$B^{m7(\flat5)}$
Min 7th up	$C^{m7(\flat5)}$	$B\flat^{m7(\flat5)}$	$A\flat^{m7(\flat5)}$	$F\#^{m7(\flat5)}$	$E^{m7(\flat5)}$	$D^{m7(\flat5)}$	$C\#^{m7(\flat5)}$	$B^{m7(\flat5)}$	$A^{m7(\flat5)}$	$G^{m7(\flat5)}$	$F^{m7(\flat5)}$	$E\flat^{m7(\flat5)}$
Min 7th down	$C^{m7(\flat5)}$	$D^{m7(\flat5)}$	$E^{m7(\flat5)}$	$F\#^{m7(\flat5)}$	$G\#^{m7(\flat5)}$	$B\flat^{m7(\flat5)}$	$C\#^{m7(\flat5)}$	$E\flat^{m7(\flat5)}$	$F^{m7(\flat5)}$	$G^{m7(\flat5)}$	$A^{m7(\flat5)}$	$B^{m7(\flat5)}$
Maj 7th up	$C^{m7(\flat5)}$	$B^{m7(\flat5)}$	$B\flat^{m7(\flat5)}$	$A^{m7(\flat5)}$	$A\flat^{m7(\flat5)}$	$G^{m7(\flat5)}$	$F\#^{m7(\flat5)}$	$F^{m7(\flat5)}$	$E^{m7(\flat5)}$	$E\flat^{m7(\flat5)}$	$D^{m7(\flat5)}$	$C\#^{m7}$
Maj 7th down	$C^{m7(\flat5)}$	$C\#^{m7(\flat5)}$	$D^{m7(\flat5)}$	$E\flat^{m7(\flat5)}$	$E^{m7(\flat5)}$	$F^{m7(\flat5)}$	$F\#^{m7(\flat5)}$	$G^{m7(\flat5)}$	$G\#^{m7(\flat5)}$	$A^{m7(\flat5)}$	$B\flat^{m7(\flat5)}$	$B^{m7(\flat5)}$

9.12. DIMINISHED 7TH CHORDS REGULAR PROGRESSIONS WORKSHEET

½ step up	C°7	C#°7	D°7	Eb°7	E°7	F°7	F#°7	G°7	G#°7	A°7	Bb°7	B°7
½ step down	C°7	B°7	Bb°7	A°7	Ab°7	G°7	F#°7	F°7	E°7	Eb°7	D°7	C#°7
Step up	C°7	D°7	E°7	F#°7	G#°7	Bb°7	C#°7	Eb°7	F°7	G°7	A°7	B°7
Step down	C°7	Bb°7	Ab°7	F#°7	E°7	D°7	C#°7	B°7	A°7	G°7	F°7	Eb°7
Min 3rd up	C°7	Eb°7	F#°7	A°7	C#°7	E°7	G°7	Bb°7	D°7	F°7	Ab°7	B°7
Min 3rd down	C°7	A°7	F#°7	Eb°7	C#°7	Bb°7	G°7	E°7	D°7	B°7	Ab°7	F°7
Maj 3rd up	C°7	E°7	G#°7	C#°7	F°7	A°7	D°7	F#°7	Bb°7	Eb°7	G°7	B°7
Maj 3rd down	C°7	G#°7	E°7	C#°7	A°7	F°7	D°7	Bb°7	F#°7	Eb°7	B°7	G°7
4th up	C°7	F°7	Bb°7	Eb°7	Ab°7	C#°7	F#°7	B°7	E°7	A°7	D°7	G°7
4th down	C°7	G°7	D°7	A°7	E°7	B°7	F#°7	C#°7	Ab°7	Eb°7	Bb°7	F°7
5th up	C°7	G°7	D°7	A°7	E°7	B°7	F#°7	C#°7	Ab°7	Eb°7	Bb°7	F°7
5th down	C°7	F°7	Bb°7	Eb°7	Abm7	C#m7	F#°7	B°7	E°7	A°7	D°7	G°7
Min 6th up	C°7	Ab°7	E°7	C#°7	A°7	F°7	D°7	Bb°7	F#°7	Eb°7	B°7	G°7
Min 6th down	C°7	E°7	G#°7	C#°7	F°7	A°7	D°7	F#°7	Bb°7	Eb°7	G°7	B°7
Maj 6th up	C°7	A°7	F#°7	Eb°7	C#°7	Bb°7	G°7	E°7	D°7	B°7	Ab°7	F°7
Maj 6th down	C°7	Eb°7	F#°7	A°7	C#°7	E°7	G°7	Bb°7	D°7	F°7	Ab°7	B°7
Min 7th up	C°7	Bb°7	Ab°7	F#°7	E°7	D°7	C#°7	B°7	A°7	G°7	F°7	Eb°7
Min 7th down	C°7	D°7	E°7	F#°7	G#°7	Bb°7	C#°7	Eb°7	F°7	G°7	A°7	B°7
Maj 7th up	C°7	B°7	Bb°7	A°7	Ab°7	G°7	F#°7	F°7	E°7	Eb°7	D°7	C#°7
Maj 7th down	C°7	C#°7	D°7	Eb°7	E°7	F°7	F#°7	G°7	G#°7	A°7	Bb°7	B°7

9.13. COPY TEMPLATES

Do not write on the templates! Use them to copy additional practice material whenever you need it.

Practice logs

	60		80		100		120		140		160		180		200		220	
C	1	2																
G																		
D																		
A																		
E																		
B																		
F#/Gb																		
Db																		
Ab																		
Eb																		
Bb																		
F																		

	60	80	100	120	140	160	180	200	220
C	1 2 3								
G									
D									
A									
E									
B									
F#/G♭									
D♭									
A♭									
E♭									
B♭									
F									

	60		80		100		120		140		160		180		200		220	
C	Ion	Mix	Ion	Mix	Ion	Mix	Ion	Mix	Ion	Mix	Ion	Mix	Ion	Mix	Ion	Mix	Ion	Mix
	Dor	Aeo	Dor	Aeo	Dor	Aeo	Dor	Aeo	Dor	Aeo	Dor	Aeo	Dor	Aeo	Dor	Aeo	Dor	Aeo
	Phr	Loc	Phr	Loc	Phr	Loc	Phr	Loc	Phr	Loc	Phr	Loc	Phr	Loc	Phr	Loc	Phr	Loc
	Lyd		Lyd		Lyd		Lyd		Lyd		Lyd		Lyd		Lyd		Lyd	
G	Ion	Mix	Ion	Mix	Ion	Mix	Ion	Mix	Ion	Mix	Ion	Mix	Ion	Mix	Ion	Mix	Ion	Mix
	Dor	Aeo	Dor	Aeo	Dor	Aeo	Dor	Aeo	Dor	Aeo	Dor	Aeo	Dor	Aeo	Dor	Aeo	Dor	Aeo
	Phr	Loc	Phr	Loc	Phr	Loc	Phr	Loc	Phr	Loc	Phr	Loc	Phr	Loc	Phr	Loc	Phr	Loc
	Lyd		Lyd		Lyd		Lyd		Lyd		Lyd		Lyd		Lyd		Lyd	
D	Ion	Mix	Ion	Mix	Ion	Mix	Ion	Mix	Ion	Mix	Ion	Mix	Ion	Mix	Ion	Mix	Ion	Mix
	Dor	Aeo	Dor	Aeo	Dor	Aeo	Dor	Aeo	Dor	Aeo	Dor	Aeo	Dor	Aeo	Dor	Aeo	Dor	Aeo
	Phr	Loc	Phr	Loc	Phr	Loc	Phr	Loc	Phr	Loc	Phr	Loc	Phr	Loc	Phr	Loc	Phr	Loc
	Lyd		Lyd		Lyd		Lyd		Lyd		Lyd		Lyd		Lyd		Lyd	
A	Ion	Mix	Ion	Mix	Ion	Mix	Ion	Mix	Ion	Mix	Ion	Mix	Ion	Mix	Ion	Mix	Ion	Mix
	Dor	Aeo	Dor	Aeo	Dor	Aeo	Dor	Aeo	Dor	Aeo	Dor	Aeo	Dor	Aeo	Dor	Aeo	Dor	Aeo
	Phr	Loc	Phr	Loc	Phr	Loc	Phr	Loc	Phr	Loc	Phr	Loc	Phr	Loc	Phr	Loc	Phr	Loc
	Lyd		Lyd		Lyd		Lyd		Lyd		Lyd		Lyd		Lyd		Lyd	
E	Ion	Mix	Ion	Mix	Ion	Mix	Ion	Mix	Ion	Mix	Ion	Mix	Ion	Mix	Ion	Mix	Ion	Mix
	Dor	Aeo	Dor	Aeo	Dor	Aeo	Dor	Aeo	Dor	Aeo	Dor	Aeo	Dor	Aeo	Dor	Aeo	Dor	Aeo
	Phr	Loc	Phr	Loc	Phr	Loc	Phr	Loc	Phr	Loc	Phr	Loc	Phr	Loc	Phr	Loc	Phr	Loc
	Lyd		Lyd		Lyd		Lyd		Lyd		Lyd		Lyd		Lyd		Lyd	
B	Ion	Mix	Ion	Mix	Ion	Mix	Ion	Mix	Ion	Mix	Ion	Mix	Ion	Mix	Ion	Mix	Ion	Mix
	Dor	Aeo	Dor	Aeo	Dor	Aeo	Dor	Aeo	Dor	Aeo	Dor	Aeo	Dor	Aeo	Dor	Aeo	Dor	Aeo
	Phr	Loc	Phr	Loc	Phr	Loc	Phr	Loc	Phr	Loc	Phr	Loc	Phr	Loc	Phr	Loc	Phr	Loc
	Lyd		Lyd		Lyd		Lyd		Lyd		Lyd		Lyd		Lyd		Lyd	
F#/G♭	Ion	Mix	Ion	Mix	Ion	Mix	Ion	Mix	Ion	Mix	Ion	Mix	Ion	Mix	Ion	Mix	Ion	Mix
	Dor	Aeo	Dor	Aeo	Dor	Aeo	Dor	Aeo	Dor	Aeo	Dor	Aeo	Dor	Aeo	Dor	Aeo	Dor	Aeo
	Phr	Loc	Phr	Loc	Phr	Loc	Phr	Loc	Phr	Loc	Phr	Loc	Phr	Loc	Phr	Loc	Phr	Loc
	Lyd		Lyd		Lyd		Lyd		Lyd		Lyd		Lyd		Lyd		Lyd	
D♭	Ion	Mix	Ion	Mix	Ion	Mix	Ion	Mix	Ion	Mix	Ion	Mix	Ion	Mix	Ion	Mix	Ion	Mix
	Dor	Aeo	Dor	Aeo	Dor	Aeo	Dor	Aeo	Dor	Aeo	Dor	Aeo	Dor	Aeo	Dor	Aeo	Dor	Aeo
	Phr	Loc	Phr	Loc	Phr	Loc	Phr	Loc	Phr	Loc	Phr	Loc	Phr	Loc	Phr	Loc	Phr	Loc
	Lyd		Lyd		Lyd		Lyd		Lyd		Lyd		Lyd		Lyd		Lyd	
A♭	Ion	Mix	Ion	Mix	Ion	Mix	Ion	Mix	Ion	Mix	Ion	Mix	Ion	Mix	Ion	Mix	Ion	Mix
	Dor	Aeo	Dor	Aeo	Dor	Aeo	Dor	Aeo	Dor	Aeo	Dor	Aeo	Dor	Aeo	Dor	Aeo	Dor	Aeo
	Phr	Loc	Phr	Loc	Phr	Loc	Phr	Loc	Phr	Loc	Phr	Loc	Phr	Loc	Phr	Loc	Phr	Loc
	Lyd		Lyd		Lyd		Lyd		Lyd		Lyd		Lyd		Lyd		Lyd	
E♭	Ion	Mix	Ion	Mix	Ion	Mix	Ion	Mix	Ion	Mix	Ion	Mix	Ion	Mix	Ion	Mix	Ion	Mix
	Dor	Aeo	Dor	Aeo	Dor	Aeo	Dor	Aeo	Dor	Aeo	Dor	Aeo	Dor	Aeo	Dor	Aeo	Dor	Aeo
	Phr	Loc	Phr	Loc	Phr	Loc	Phr	Loc	Phr	Loc	Phr	Loc	Phr	Loc	Phr	Loc	Phr	Loc
	Lyd		Lyd		Lyd		Lyd		Lyd		Lyd		Lyd		Lyd		Lyd	
B♭	Ion	Mix	Ion	Mix	Ion	Mix	Ion	Mix	Ion	Mix	Ion	Mix	Ion	Mix	Ion	Mix	Ion	Mix
	Dor	Aeo	Dor	Aeo	Dor	Aeo	Dor	Aeo	Dor	Aeo	Dor	Aeo	Dor	Aeo	Dor	Aeo	Dor	Aeo
	Phr	Loc	Phr	Loc	Phr	Loc	Phr	Loc	Phr	Loc	Phr	Loc	Phr	Loc	Phr	Loc	Phr	Loc
	Lyd		Lyd		Lyd		Lyd		Lyd		Lyd		Lyd		Lyd		Lyd	
F	Ion	Mix	Ion	Mix	Ion	Mix	Ion	Mix	Ion	Mix	Ion	Mix	Ion	Mix	Ion	Mix	Ion	Mix
	Dor	Aeo	Dor	Aeo	Dor	Aeo	Dor	Aeo	Dor	Aeo	Dor	Aeo	Dor	Aeo	Dor	Aeo	Dor	Aeo
	Phr	Loc	Phr	Loc	Phr	Loc	Phr	Loc	Phr	Loc	Phr	Loc	Phr	Loc	Phr	Loc	Phr	Loc
	Lyd		Lyd		Lyd		Lyd		Lyd		Lyd		Lyd		Lyd		Lyd	

	60		80		100		120		140		160		180		200		220	
C	1	5	1	5	1	5	1	5	1	5	1	5	1	5	1	5	1	5
	2	6	2	6	2	6	2	6	2	6	2	6	2	6	2	6	2	6
	3	7	3	7	3	7	3	7	3	7	3	7	3	7	3	7	3	7
	4		4		4		4		4		4		4		4		4	
G	1	5	1	5	1	5	1	5	1	5	1	5	1	5	1	5	1	5
	2	6	2	6	2	6	2	6	2	6	2	6	2	6	2	6	2	6
	3	7	3	7	3	7	3	7	3	7	3	7	3	7	3	7	3	7
	4		4		4		4		4		4		4		4		4	
D	1	5	1	5	1	5	1	5	1	5	1	5	1	5	1	5	1	5
	2	6	2	6	2	6	2	6	2	6	2	6	2	6	2	6	2	6
	3	7	3	7	3	7	3	7	3	7	3	7	3	7	3	7	3	7
	4		4		4		4		4		4		4		4		4	
A	1	5	1	5	1	5	1	5	1	5	1	5	1	5	1	5	1	5
	2	6	2	6	2	6	2	6	2	6	2	6	2	6	2	6	2	6
	3	7	3	7	3	7	3	7	3	7	3	7	3	7	3	7	3	7
	4		4		4		4		4		4		4		4		4	
E	1	5	1	5	1	5	1	5	1	5	1	5	1	5	1	5	1	5
	2	6	2	6	2	6	2	6	2	6	2	6	2	6	2	6	2	6
	3	7	3	7	3	7	3	7	3	7	3	7	3	7	3	7	3	7
	4		4		4		4		4		4		4		4		4	
B	1	5	1	5	1	5	1	5	1	5	1	5	1	5	1	5	1	5
	2	6	2	6	2	6	2	6	2	6	2	6	2	6	2	6	2	6
	3	7	3	7	3	7	3	7	3	7	3	7	3	7	3	7	3	7
	4		4		4		4		4		4		4		4		4	
F#/Gb	1	5	1	5	1	5	1	5	1	5	1	5	1	5	1	5	1	5
	2	6	2	6	2	6	2	6	2	6	2	6	2	6	2	6	2	6
	3	7	3	7	3	7	3	7	3	7	3	7	3	7	3	7	3	7
	4		4		4		4		4		4		4		4		4	
Db	1	5	1	5	1	5	1	5	1	5	1	5	1	5	1	5	1	5
	2	6	2	6	2	6	2	6	2	6	2	6	2	6	2	6	2	6
	3	7	3	7	3	7	3	7	3	7	3	7	3	7	3	7	3	7
	4		4		4		4		4		4		4		4		4	
Ab	1	5	1	5	1	5	1	5	1	5	1	5	1	5	1	5	1	5
	2	6	2	6	2	6	2	6	2	6	2	6	2	6	2	6	2	6
	3	7	3	7	3	7	3	7	3	7	3	7	3	7	3	7	3	7
	4		4		4		4		4		4		4		4		4	
Eb	1	5	1	5	1	5	1	5	1	5	1	5	1	5	1	5	1	5
	2	6	2	6	2	6	2	6	2	6	2	6	2	6	2	6	2	6
	3	7	3	7	3	7	3	7	3	7	3	7	3	7	3	7	3	7
	4		4		4		4		4		4		4		4		4	
Bb	1	5	1	5	1	5	1	5	1	5	1	5	1	5	1	5	1	5
	2	6	2	6	2	6	2	6	2	6	2	6	2	6	2	6	2	6
	3	7	3	7	3	7	3	7	3	7	3	7	3	7	3	7	3	7
	4		4		4		4		4		4		4		4		4	
F	1	5	1	5	1	5	1	5	1	5	1	5	1	5	1	5	1	5
	2	6	2	6	2	6	2	6	2	6	2	6	2	6	2	6	2	6
	3	7	3	7	3	7	3	7	3	7	3	7	3	7	3	7	3	7
	4		4		4		4		4		4		4		4		4	

Empty Staffs

Empty AABA Form

Empty Blues Form

9.14. ALTERNATE CHORD SYMBOLS

Triads

		Alternate chord symbols:
Major triad	C	CM, C$\triangle$, Cmaj, C^M, C$^\triangle$, C^{maj}
Minor triad	Cm	C-, Cmin, C^{min}
Augmented triad	C+	Caug, C^{aug}
Diminished triad	C°	Cdim, C^{dim}

Seventh chords

Major seventh	Cmaj7	CMaj7, C$\triangle$7, C^{maj7}, C^{maj7}, C$^\triangle$7
Dominant seventh	C7	C7, Cdom7, C^{dom7}
Minor seventh	Cm7	Cm7, Cmin7, C^{m7}, C^{m7}, C^{min7}
Minor seventh (♭5) (Half-diminished seventh)	Cm7(♭5)	Cm7(♭5), Cmin7(♭5), Cm7♭5, Cm7$^{♭5}$, Cmin7$^{♭5}$, C$^\emptyset$, C$^{\emptyset7}$, C$^\emptyset$7
Diminished seventh	C°7	Cdim7, Cdim7, C°7, C$^{°7}$
Augmented seventh	C7(♯5)	C7$^{♯5}$, C$^{7(♯5)}$, C+7, C^{+7}, Caug7, C^{aug7}

Ninth chords

Major ninth	Cmaj9	C$^{\triangle9}$, CMaj7(9), C$^{maj7(9)}$
Dominant ninth	C9	C^9, C7(9), C7^9, C$^{7(9)}$, Cdom9
Dominant (♭9)	C7(♭9)	C7$^{♭9}$, C$^{7(♭9)}$
Augmented ninth	C9(♯5)	C+7(9), C+7^9, C$^{+7(9)}$, Caug7(9), C$^{aug7(9)}$
Augmented dominant (♭9)	C7(♯5, ♭9)	C+7(♭9), C+7$^{♭9}$, C+$^{7(♭9)}$
Minor ninth	Cm9	Cm^9, C-9, C-^{9}, Cmin9
Minor ninth (♭5)	Cm9(♭5)	Cm7(♭5, 9), Cm7$^{(♭5, 9)}$, Cmin7$^{(♭5, 9)}$, Cmin9(♭5)

Eleventh chords		Alternate chord symbols:
Major ninth (#11)	Cmaj9(#11)	Cmaj7$^{(9,\,\sharp11)}$, C$\triangle$7$^{(9,\,\sharp11)}$
Dominant eleventh	C11	C^{11}, Cdom11, C7$^{(9,\,11)}$
Dominant ninth (#11)	C9(#11)	C7$^{(9,\,\sharp11)}$, Cdom9$^{(\sharp11)}$
Dominant ninth (#5, #11)	C9(#5, #11)	C+7$^{(9,\,\sharp11)}$, C$^{aug7(9,\,\sharp11)}$
Minor eleventh	Cm11	Cm7(9, 11), Cmin7$^{(9,\,11)}$
Minor eleventh (♭5)	Cm11(♭5)	Cmin7$^{(\flat5,\,9,\,11)}$, C$^{\o7(9,\,11)}$
Thirteenth chords		
Major thirteenth (#11)	Cmaj13(#11)	C$\triangle$7$^{(9,\,\sharp11,\,13)}$, Cmaj7$^{(9,\,\sharp11,\,13)}$
Dominant thirteenth (#11)	C13(#11)	C7$^{(9,\,\sharp11,\,13)}$, C13$^{(9,\,\sharp11)}$, Cdom13$^{(9,\,\sharp11)}$
Dominant thirteenth (♭9, #11)	C13(♭9, #11)	C7(♭9, #11, 13), C13(b9, #11), Cdom13(♭9, #11)
Minor thirteenth	Cm13	Cm^{13}, C-13, C-^{13}, Cmin13
Minor seventh (♭9, ♭13)	Cm7(♭9, ♭13)	Cmin7$^{(\flat9,\,\flat13)}$, Cm7$^{(\flat9,\,\flat13)}$
Minor seventh (♭5, ♭13)	Cm7(♭5, ♭13)	Cmin7$^{(\flat5,\,\flat13)}$, C$^{\o7(\flat5,\,\flat13)}$
Minor seventh (♭5, ♭9, ♭13)	Cm7(♭5, ♭9, ♭13)	Cmin7$^{(\flat5,\,\flat9,\,\flat13)}$, C$^{\o7(\flat5,\,\flat9,\,\flat13)}$

This is not a complete list!

9.15. GOAL-ORIENTED PRACTICING

Setting goals makes it easier to understand where you are going. Goals also allow you to measure and feel progress. At first, it may be hard to find the goals you want to achieve. It is a good idea to consult a music teacher or a friend who is a more advanced player to discuss possible goals.

Start with long-term goals, picturing where you want to be in five years. Then decide on medium-term goals that break down the long-term goals in smaller units (one year). Short-term goals and daily goals are more detailed goals that are easier to achieve.

The following two pages will help you track your goals.

Goal-Oriented Practicing

Today's date: _____

5 years
This is what I want to be able to play on my saxophone in five years:

-

-

-

1 year
This is what I want to be able to play on my saxophone in one year:

-

-

-

6 months
This is what I want to be able to play on my saxophone in six months:

-

-

-

1 month
This is what I want to be able to play on my saxophone in one month:

-

-

-

Weekly Practice Schedule

Year _____ / Week _____

Monday
•
•
•

Tuesday
•
•
•

Wednesday
•
•
•

Thursday
•
•
•

Friday
•
•
•

Saturday
•
•
•

Sunday
•
•
•

❑ This was a great practice week!

❑ This was a good practice week.

❑ This was an okay practice week.

❑ This was a lousy practice week.

9.16. ANALYTICAL LISTENING

The personal style of a saxophone player is a combination of his or her vocabulary, tone, articulation, melodic and harmonic concept, use of vibrato and other effects, time and swing feel, and repertoire, as well as other things. A key element for the development of your own personal style and musical growth is understanding how great players use these music aspects.

The following checklist allows you to track when you listen to great saxophone players (i.e. chapter assignments). Check the boxes relating to the sound of each musician you listen to.

Name of the saxophone player: _____

Tone

☐ airy   ☐ bright   ☐ clean   ☐ big   ☐ light

☐ nasal   ☐ small   ☐ classical   ☐ open   ☐ dark

☐ round   ☐ mellow   ☐ edgy   ☐ thin   ☐ fat

☐ dry   ☐ focused   ☐ angry   ☐ cheerful   ☐ calm

☐ dramatic   ☐ tense   ☐ stiff   ☐ loose

Articulation

☐ plays mostly slurred   ☐ plays ghost notes

☐ plays mostly tongued   ☐ uses great variety of articulation

☐ uses upbeat tonguing   ☐ uses little variety of articulation

☐ uses consecutive tonguing   ☐ tongues notes heavily

☐ tongues notes lightly

Vibrato

☐ uses vibrato frequently   ☐ uses vibrato rarely

☐ fast vibrato   ☐ slow vibrato

☐ extreme vibrato (width)   ☐ modest vibrato (width)

☐ "fade out" vibrato   ☐ classical vibrato

Technique

☐ great   ☐ advanced but not great   ☐ unusual

☐ clean   ☐ loose

Effects

- ☐ breathing noise
- ☐ finger clicking
- ☐ key clapping
- ☐ "laughing"
- ☐ triple tonguing
- ☐ multiphonics
- ☐ bending
- ☐ false fingerings
- ☐ vibrato
- ☐ trills
- ☐ electronic effects
- ☐ flutter tonguing
- ☐ altissimo register
- ☐ biting
- ☐ ghost notes
- ☐ growling
- ☐ quarter tones
- ☐ double tonguing
- ☐ harmonics/overtones
- ☐ circular breathing
- ☐ rips

Rhythm

- ☐ extensive rhythmic vocabulary
- ☐ repeats patterns
- ☐ plays long phrases
- ☐ limited rhythmic vocabulary
- ☐ plays double time
- ☐ plays short phrases
- ☐ uses polyrhythms
- ☐ uses a lot of rest

Swing feel

- ☐ swings eighth notes
- ☐ plays even eighth notes
- ☐ swings sixteenth notes
- ☐ accents on downbeat
- ☐ triplet feel
- ☐ accents on upbeat

Time feel

- ☐ on the beat   ☐ behind   ☐ on top   ☐ floating

Use of melody

- ☐ scales
- ☐ chord tones
- ☐ appoggiaturas
- ☐ sequences
- ☐ common intervals
- ☐ embellishments
- ☐ quotes
- ☐ personal licks
- ☐ motives
- ☐ approach tones
- ☐ patterns
- ☐ clichés

Use of harmony

- ☐ outlines harmony linearly
- ☐ stays diatonic to key(s)
- ☐ follows harmonic rhythm
- ☐ reharmonizes
- ☐ uses tensions
- ☐ uses chromaticism
- ☐ plays harmony vertically (up and down)
- ☐ plays outside of key(s)
- ☐ plays beyond harmonic rhythm
- ☐ uses chord tones
- ☐ anticipates chord changes

Repertoire

- ☐ Ragtime
- ☐ Blues
- ☐ Swing
- ☐ Dixieland
- ☐ Afro-Cuban Jazz
- ☐ Cool Jazz
- ☐ Bebop
- ☐ Modal Jazz
- ☐ Hard Bop
- ☐ Latin Jazz
- ☐ Soul Jazz
- ☐ Fusion
- ☐ Jazz Rock
- ☐ Smooth Jazz
- ☐ Psychedelic Jazz
- ☐ Funk
- ☐ Acid Jazz
- ☐ Third Stream
- ☐ Originals
- ☐ Standards
- ☐ Free Jazz

CHAPTER TEST SOLUTIONS

Chapter 1
A1: W W H W W W H

A2: Dorian

A3: Aeolian

A4: Eb, F, G, Ab, Bb, C, D, and Eb

A5: B, C#, D#, E, F#, G#, A#, and B

A6: D, E, F#, G, A, B, C, and D

A7: F, Gb, Ab, Bb, C, Db, Eb, and F

A8: F#, A, and C

A9: Db, F, A

A10: Second inversion

Chapter 2
A1: 1 2 b3 4 5 b6 7 8

A2: E, F#, G, A, B, C, D#, and E

A3: Ab, Bb, Cb, Db, Eb, Fb, G, and Ab

A4: B, C#, D, E, F#, G, A#, and B

A5: Romanian

A6: Phrygian dominant

A7: Harmonic minor

A8: D, F, and A

A9: Ab, F, and C

A10: G, C, and Eb

Chapter 3
A1: 1 2 b3 4 5 6 7 8

A2: E, F#, G, A, B, C#, D#, and E

A3: Db, Eb, Fb, Gb, Ab, Bb, C, and Db

A4: F#, G#, A, B, C#, D#, E#, and F#

A5: C, E, and G#

A6: Bb, Db, and Fb

A7: A, C#, and E#

A8: G, Bb, and Db

A9: Dorian b9

A10: Lydian augmented

Chapter 4
A1: H H H H H H H H H H H H

A2: Eb, G, Bb, and D

A3: F#, A#, C#, and E

A4: Bb, Db, F, and Ab

A5: G, Bb, Db, and F

A6: D, F, Ab, and Cb

A7: F, A, C#, and Eb

A8: Ab, Cb, Eb, and G

A9: C, E, G, and A

A10: E, G, B, and C#

Chapter 5
A1: Gb, Ab, Bb, Db, Eb, and Gb

A2: B, D, E, F#, A, and B

A3: A tension nine implies that there is a seventh in the chord.

A4: C, E, G, B, and D

A5: Eb, G, Bb, Db, and F

A6: A, C#, E, G, and Bb

A7: F, A, C#, Eb, and G

A8: Bb, D, F#, Ab, and Cb

A9: G, Bb, D, F, and A

A10: Db, Fb, Abb, Cb, and Eb

Chapter 6

A1:   1 x ♭3 4 ♭5 5 x ♭7 8

A2:   A, C, D, E♭, E, G, and A

A3:   E, G, A, B♭, B, D, and E

A4:   F♯, A, B, C, C♯, E, and F♯

A5:   B♭, D, F, A, C, and E

A6:   C, E, G, B♭, D, and F

A7:   F, A, C, E♭, G, and B

A8:   G, B, D♯, F, A, and C♯

A9:   E♭, G♭, B♭, D♭, F, and A♭

A10: D, F, A♭, C, E, and G

Chapter 7

A1:   D♭, E♭, F, G, A, B, and D♭

A2:   G, A, A♯/B♭, C, C♯/D♭, E♭, E, F♯/G♭, and G

A3:   D♯, E, F♯, G, A, B, C, D, and D♯

A4:   A♭, C, E♭, G, B♭, D, and F

A5:   F, A, C, E♭, G, B, and D

A6:   E, G♯, B, D, F, A♯, and C♯

A7:   F♯, A, C♯, E, G♯, B, and D♯

A8:   B, D, F♯, A, C, E, and G

A9:   A, C, E♭, G, B, D, and F

A10: C, E♭, G♭, B♭, D♭, F, and A♭

Chapter 8

A1:   B, C♯, D♯, E, F♯, G♯, A, A♯, and B

A2:   D♭, E♭, F, G♭, A♭, B♭, B/C♭, C, and D♭

A3:   G, A, B♭, B, C, D, E, F, and G

A4:   E, F♯, G, G♯, A, B, C♯, D, and E

A5:   A♭, B♭, C, D♭, E♭, E, F, G, and A♭

A6:   F, G, A, B♭, C, C♯, D, E, and F

A7:   B♭, C, D♭, E♭, F, F♯, G, A, and B♭

A8:   D, E, F, G, A, A♯, B, C♯, and D

A9:   A, B, C, D, E, F, G, G♯, and A

A10: Thank you very much for your effort, time, and interest! Keep up the good work!

Hal·Leonard®
SAXOPHONE PLAY-ALONG

The Saxophone Play-Along Series will help you play your favorite songs quickly and easily. Just follow the music, listen to the audio to hear how the saxophone should sound, and then play along using the separate backing tracks. Each song is printed twice in the book: once for alto and once for tenor saxes. The melody and lyrics are also included. The online audio is available for streaming or download using the unique code printed inside the book, and it includes **PLAYBACK+** options such as looping and tempo adjustments.

1. ROCK 'N' ROLL
Bony Moronie • Charlie Brown • Hand Clappin' • Honky Tonk (Parts 1 & 2) • I'm Walkin' • Lucille (You Won't Do Your Daddy's Will) • See You Later, Alligator • Shake, Rattle and Roll.
00113137 Book/Online Audio $16.99

2. R&B
Cleo's Mood • I Got a Woman • Pick up the Pieces • Respect • Shot Gun • Soul Finger • Soul Serenade • Unchain My Heart.
00113177 Book/Online Audio $16.99

3. CLASSIC ROCK
Baker Street • Deacon Blues • The Heart of Rock and Roll • Jazzman • Smooth Operator • Turn the Page • Who Can It Be Now? • Young Americans.
00113429 Book/Online Audio $16.99

4. SAX CLASSICS
Boulevard of Broken Dreams • Harlem Nocturne • Night Train • Peter Gunn • The Pink Panther • St. Thomas • Tequila • Yakety Sax.
00114393 Book/Online Audio. $16.99

5. CHARLIE PARKER
Billie's Bounce (Bill's Bounce) • Confirmation • Dewey Square • Donna Lee • Now's the Time • Ornithology • Scrapple from the Apple • Yardbird Suite.
00118286 Book/Online Audio...$16.99

6. DAVE KOZ
All I See Is You • Can't Let You Go (The Sha La Song) • Emily • Honey-Dipped • Know You by Heart • Put the Top Down • Together Again • You Make Me Smile.
00118292 Book/Online Audio $16.99

7. GROVER WASHINGTON, JR.
East River Drive • Just the Two of Us • Let It Flow • Make Me a Memory (Sad Samba) • Mr. Magic • Take Five • Take Me There • Winelight.
00118293 Book/Online Audio $16.99

8. DAVID SANBORN
Anything You Want • Bang Bang • Chicago Song • Comin' Home Baby • The Dream • Hideaway • Slam • Straight to the Heart.
00125694 Book/Online Audio $16.99

9. CHRISTMAS
The Christmas Song (Chestnuts Roasting on an Open Fire) • Christmas Time Is Here • Count Your Blessings Instead of Sheep • Do You Hear What I Hear • Have Yourself a Merry Little Christmas • The Little Drummer Boy • White Christmas • Winter Wonderland.
00148170 Book/Online Audio $16.99

10. JOHN COLTRANE
Blue Train (Blue Trane) • Body and Soul • Central Park West • Cousin Mary • Giant Steps • Like Sonny (Simple Like) • My Favorite Things • Naima (Niema).
00193333 Book/Online Audio $16.99

11. JAZZ ICONS
Body and Soul • Con Alma • Oleo • Speak No Evil • Take Five • There Will Never Be Another You • Tune Up • Work Song.
00199296 Book/Online Audio $16.99

HAL·LEONARD®

Visit Hal Leonard online at **www.halleonard.com**

Prices, contents, and availability subject to change without notice. 0417

SAXOPHONE
IMPROVE YOUR TECHNIQUE

AMANZING PHRASING
50 WAYS TO IMPROVE YOUR IMPROVISATIONAL SKILLS
by Dennis Taylor
Amazing Phrasing is for any sax player interested in learning how to improvise and how to improve their creative phrasing. The ideas are divided into three sections: harmony, rhythm, and melody. The companion audio includes full-band tracks in various musical styles for listening and play along.
00311108 Alto Sax, Book/CD Pack............... $17.95
00310787 Tenor Sax, Book/Online Audio...... $16.99

PAUL DESMOND
A STEP-BY-STEP BREAKDOWN OF THE SAX STYLES AND TECHNIQUES OF A JAZZ GREAT
by Eric J. Morones
Examine the sophisticated sounds of a jazz sax legend with this instructional pack that explores 12 Desmond classics: Alone Together • Any Other Time • Bossa Antigua • I've Got You Under My Skin • Jazzabelle • Take Five • Take Ten • Time After Time • and more.
00695983 Book/CD Pack $19.99

JAZZ SAXOPHONE
AN IN-DEPTH LOOK AT THE STYLES OF THE TENOR MASTERS
by Dennis Taylor
All the best are here: from the cool bebop excursions of Dexter Gordon, to the stellar musings of John Coltrane, with more than a dozen master players examined in between. Includes lessons, music, historical analysis and rare photos, plus a CD with 16 full-band tracks!
00310983 Book/CD Pack $18.95

MODERN SAXOPHONE TECHNIQUES
by Frank Catalano
Many books present facts, but this guude teaches the developing player how to learn. Listening, exploring, writing original music, and trial and error are some of the methods threaded throughout. On the online video, author and virtuoso saxophonist Frank Catalano offers quick tips on many of the topics covered in the book. Topics include: developing good rhythm • air stream and embouchure • fingering charts • tonguing techniques • modern harmony tips • and more.
00123829 Book/Online Video $24.99

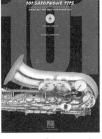

101 SAXOPHONE TIPS
by Eric Morones
This book presents valuable how-to insight that saxophone players of all styles and levels can benefit from. The text, photos, music, diagrams, and accompanying CD provide a terrific, easy-to-use resource for a variety of topics, including: techniques; maintenance; equipment; practicing; recording; performance; and much more!
00311082 Book/CD Pack $14.95

SONNY ROLLINS
A STEP-BY-STEP BREAKDOWN OF THE SAX STYLES & TECHNIQUES OF A JAZZ GIANT
Explore the unique sound and soul of jazz innovator Sonny Rollins on licks from 12 classic songs: Airegin • Biji • Don't Stop the Carnival • Doxy • Duke of Iron • God Bless' the Child • Oleo • St. Thomas • Sonnymoon for Two • Tenor Madness • Way Out West • You Don't Know What Love Is.
00695854 Book/CD Pack $19.99

SAXOPHONE AEROBICS
by Woody Mankowski
This 52-week, one-exercise-a-day workout program for developing, improving and maintaining saxophone technique includes access to demo audio tracks online for all 365 workout licks! Techniques covered include: scales • articulations • rhythms • range extension • arpeggios • ornaments • and stylings. Benefits of using this book include: facile technique • better intonation • increased style vocabulary • heightened rhythmic acuity • improved ensemble playing • and expanded range.
00143344 Book/Online Audio $19.99

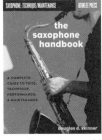

THE SAXOPHONE HANDBOOK
COMPLETE GUIDE TO TONE, TECHNIQUE, AND PERFORMANCE
by Douglas D. Skinner
Berklee Press
A complete guide to playing and maintenance, this handbook offers essential information on all dimensions of the saxophone. It provides an overview of technique, such as breathing, fingerings, articulations, and more. Exercises will help you develop your sense of timing, facility, and sound. You'll learn to fine-tune your reed, recork the keys, fix binding keys, replace pads, and many other repairs and adjustments. You'll also learn to improve your tone, intonation, and flexibility while playing with proper technique.
50449658 .... $14.99

SAXOPHONE SOUND EFFECTS
by Ueli Dörig
Berklee Press
Add unique saxophone sounds to your palette of colors! The saxophone is capable of a great range of sounds, from laughs and growls to multiphonics and percussion effects. This book shows you how to do 19 different inventive effects, with etudes that put them in a musical context. The accompanying online audio provides play-along tracks for the etudes and examples of each sound effect in isolation.
50449628 Book/Online Audio $15.99

SAXOPHONE WORKOUT
by Eric J. Morones
This book will give you a complete saxophone workout. Here you'll find etudes that cover a wide spectrum of techniques, from the basics to intermeidate level to advanced. With daily practice that includes use of a metronome and tuner, this book will provide noticeable improvement in the mastery of your horn. The excercises are designed for the trouble spots of all the instruments of the saxophone family – soprano, alto, tenor, baritone – and can be used by players at all levels.
00121478 .... $12.99

25 GREAT SAX SOLOS
TRANSCRIPTIONS • LESSONS • BIOS • PHOTOS
by Eric J. Morones
From Chuck Rio and King Curtis to David Sanborn and Kenny G, take an inside look at the genesis of pop saxophone. This book with online audio provides solo transcriptions in standard notation, lessons on how to play them, bios, equipment, photos, history, and much more. The audio contains full-band demos of every sax solo in the book, and includes the PLAYBACK+ audio player which allows you to adjust the recording to any tempo without changing pitch, loop challenging parts, pan, and more! Songs include: After the Love Has Gone • Deacon Blues • Just the Two of Us • Just the Way You Are • Mercy, Mercy Me • Money • Respect • Spooky • Take Five • Tequila • Yakety Sax • and more.
00311315 Book/Online Audio $19.99

HAL•LEONARD®
www.halleonard.com

0717

ARTIST TRANSCRIPTIONS

Artist Transcriptions are authentic, note-for-note transcriptions of today's hottest artists in jazz, pop and rock. These outstanding, accurate arrangements are in an easy-to-read format which includes all essential lines. **Artist Transcriptions** can be used to perform, sequence or for reference.